Saigon: Year of the Cat

SAIGON

YEAR OF THE CAT

A Film for Television

DAVID HARE

faber and faber
LONDON · BOSTON

First published in 1983
by Faber and Faber Limited
3 Queen Square London WC1N 3AU
Filmset by Wilmaset Birkenhead
Printed in Great Britain by
Redwood Burn Limited Trowbridge
All rights reserved

© *David Hare, 1983*

All rights whatsoever in this play are
strictly reserved and applications for
permission to perform it, etc., must be
made in advance, before rehearsals begin,
to Margaret Ramsay Ltd, 14a Goodwin's
Court, St Martin's Lane, London WC2

British Library Cataloguing in Publication Data

Hare, David
  Saigon.
  I. Title
  822'.914   PR6058.A678

  ISBN 0-571-11980-8

The publication of *Saigon* gives me a chance to thank the US/UK Bicentennial Committee for a Fellowship that allowed me to spend most of 1978 in the USA. *Saigon* is, essentially, the result of that visit. The making of a film on this subject and on this scale depends on the skill and enthusiasm of a great many people, of whom I must particularly thank Verity Lambert, Michael Dunlop and Stephen Frears. The accuracy of my view of Saigon was checked by a number of experts to whom I am similarly grateful, as I am to Michael and Catriona Cook who were my hosts during my original visit to Vietnam. I am sure everyone involved will nevertheless forgive my dedication: to Lewis, my son.

D.H.

CHARACTERS

At the Bank:
BARBARA DEAN
MR HALIWELL
QUOC
DONALD HENDERSON
LHAN
PHU
Tellers, Customers etc.

At the Embassy:
BOB CHESNEAU
JACK OCKHAM
FRANK JUDD
JOAN MACKINTOSH
COLONEL FIEDLER
LINDA
THE AMBASSADOR
Secretaries, Officers, GIs etc.

Elsewhere:
VAN TRANG
NHIEU
BRAD
BARBARA'S MAID
Waiters, Bar Girls, People of Saigon

Saigon: Year of the Cat was first shown on Thames Television in November 1983. The principal parts were played as follows:

BARBARA DEAN	Judi Dench
BOB CHESNEAU	Frederic Forrest
QUOC	Pitchit Bulkul
THE AMBASSADOR	E. G. Marshall
JACK OCKHAM	Josef Sommer
FRANK JUDD	Wallace Shawn
DONALD HENDERSON	Roger Rees
MR HALIWELL	Chic Murray
COLONEL FIEDLER	Manning Redwood
JOAN MACKINTOSH	Thomasine Heiner
NHIEU	Po Pau Pee
PRESIDENT THIEU	Thavisakdi Srimuang
Director	Stephen Frears
Producers	Verity Lambert
	Michael Dunlop

PART ONE

1. INT. LIVING ROOM. DAY

We are tracking through Barbara's apartment in the largely diplomatic section of Saigon. The blinds are all down against the fierce sun outside. It is dark and quiet and looks cool. There is a little plain furniture in good taste. The living room is bare-floored, tidy, the chairs in plain wood with white cushions. As we move through, we hear Barbara's voice.

BARBARA: (VO) Afternoons have always hit me the hardest, I
    don't know why that is, it's always been so. . . .

2. INT. BEDROOM. DAY

Into the bedroom, continuous, past the door jamb. We can make out very little, except slits of light across blinds at the end of the room. There is a dim lamp on beside a double bed on which BARBARA *lies. We track nearer.*

BARBARA: (VO) Mornings are fine, there's something to look
    forward to, and evenings, yes, I begin to cheer up. . . .
    (*In the bed* BARBARA *is lying bunched sideways, not really
    reading the paperback in her hand. She is in a cream slip,
    covered by a sheet. She is almost 50 and blonde. She has the
    quietness and reserve of the genteel English middle class, but in
    her it has a pleasantness which is definitely erotic. She is sweating
    slightly as we approach.*)
    (VO) But what would I wish for if I could wish for anything?
    This would be my wish: abolish afternoons.

3. EXT. TU DO. DAY

Later. After her siesta, BARBARA *in a linen dress walking down the*

busy street at the centre of Saigon. Shops, cyclists, the low blue taxis.
The Vietnamese selling food and American PX goods on the sidewalk.
BARBARA: (VO) It was never my intention my life should be
secretive, it came about by accident, I think. . . .
(She goes into a small newsagent's.)
My first affair was with a friend of my father's, so really the
style was adopted from then.
(She reappears with the airmail edition of The Times, and
walks on down the street.)
People say, 'Barbara, I've never known anyone so secretive.'
But it's only something which has happened with the years.

4. INT. HALIWELL'S OFFICE. EVENING
A Victorian-seeming office with a fan above. HALIWELL working at a
mahogany desk. Behind him, a large old-fashioned safe and wooden
filing cabinets. He is in his late fifties with some silver hair left. A
bachelor, fattening slightly, in a cotton shirt.
BARBARA: Mr Haliwell.
HALIWELL: Barbara. A satisfactory siesta?
BARBARA: Fine. I collected the paper.
HALIWELL: Ah thanks.
(He looks up. A routine.)
Any news of the Arsenal?
BARBARA: I haven't looked. The sport's on page ten.

5. INT. BANK. EVENING
An old-fashioned commercial bank. Busy. Vaulted ceilings.
Grandeur. Fans. The Vietnamese sitting behind iron grilles, serving a
clientele of Asians and whites. Beyond the grilles, a large open area
where the desks of the more senior staff are set out. A CLIENT is being
ushered in to meet BARBARA by QUOC, a tall, thin, grave Vietnamese in
his late forties, who wears grey flannel trousers and a short-sleeved
shirt. The client is named TRINH.
BARBARA: Hello.
(She shakes TRINH's hand and gestures him to sit opposite her.
QUOC brings round documents to her side of the desk and puts
them down.)

Mr Quoc has explained your application. You have good collateral.

TRINH: Yes.

BARBARA: You're securing the loan with the rest of your cargo fleet?

QUOC: Mr Trinh has fifty ships between here and Punan.
(QUOC *has confirmed this by discreetly referring to a paper which* BARBARA *has in the file in front of her. She smiles warmly at* TRINH *and begins to write on the file.*)

BARBARA: In that case I can't see there'll be any problem.

QUOC: (*Discreetly again, on* TRINH'*s behalf*) Mr Trinh is only worried about time. How long we may give him for repayment.

BARBARA: (*Quietly, not looking up*) I'm not giving anyone more than a year.

6. INT. BANK. EVENING

The bank now deserted, BARBARA *tidying her desk. Beyond her the door to Haliwell's office is open and* HENDERSON *is packing away the contents of the safe for the night. He is a young Scot about 25, with a beard, very lean. He is talking from the other room.*

HENDERSON: That's the bastard of supporting St Mirren, they don't always have the result in *The Times*.
(BARBARA *gets up to go.*)
It's Scotland who go on producing the players, but when you look for coverage, it's Leeds, Leeds, Leeds. I mean, it's ridiculous, they're all Scottish players . . .

BARBARA: Yes, it's tricky I see.

HENDERSON: That and economic misfortune. It's barely worth reading the thing any more.
(*She has gone to the main door and is about to open it to leave.* HENDERSON *has appeared at the door of Haliwell's office. He speaks from right across the bank.*)
Barbara . . .

BARBARA: Yes?

HENDERSON: Are you free for this evening? I was hoping we'd be able to go out. It's been some time.

(There's a pause. He looks down, a little embarrassed. Then with some personal feeling:)
It was wonderful last time.
(She looks at him, straight across the bank, her manners perfect.)
BARBARA: Oh Donald, I'm sorry. I'm busy tonight.

7. INT. CERCLE SPORTIF. NIGHT
The main lounge of the Cercle Sportif. A French colonial club. A large central room, bamboo armchairs, white-coated servants with trays. BARBARA *stands at the main entrance, dressed smartly but lightly for the evening.* FRANK JUDD, *a fat, bespectacled 32-year-old American in seersuckers and short-sleeved shirt, moves across at once to greet her.*
JUDD: Barbara. Hi.
BARBARA: Frank. How are you?
JUDD: Come and meet the rest.
(They have arrived next to two men who are sitting drinking. They now stand up. COLONEL FIEDLER *is a powerfully built American army officer of 55, in uniform.* VAN TRANG *is a small fat Vietnamese of the same age, in a shiny black suit.)*
Barbara Dean. You know the Foreign Minister, Monsieur Van Trang?
(They smile and shake hands.)
Barbara. Colonel Fiedler.
BARBARA: How do you do?
(They also shake hands.)
JUDD: The Colonel's just back this evening from Binh Dinh.
BARBARA: Oh really? How are things going up there?
JUDD: I think you'll find him a very good partner.
BARBARA: Well I hope so.
(The COLONEL *smiles.)*
COLONEL: Are they ready for us yet?

8. INT. CERCLE SPORTIF. NIGHT
An annexe of the main lounge. Darker. Green baize tables have been set out for cards. BARBARA, *the* COLONEL, JUDD *and* VAN TRANG

14

sitting as three servants lay out their drinks and unwrap fresh packs of cards for them.

JUDD: The Foreign Minister plays an orthodox Acol.

(BARBARA *smiles at the* COLONEL.)

BARBARA: I play a forcing two clubs.

COLONEL: No doubt we'll get the hang of each other.

JUDD: Good. Let's cut for the deal.

(*A polite cut is silently made. The* COLONEL *starts to deal, as the* MINISTER *makes formal conversation.*)

VAN TRANG: I have not been in England for too long a time.

BARBARA: No, well, I haven't been back.

VAN TRANG: Both my daughters are at Cheltenham Ladies' College.

BARBARA: Ah, well, I'm told it's a very good school.

(*She smiles and looks away to the main lounge. There a couple of bar girls have appeared, conspicuous in the otherwise discreet surroundings. They wear short slit skirts and heavy make-up. Everyone else ignores them.*)

VAN TRANG: I wish I got more chance to visit them. I am told Sports Day is the highlight of the year.

(JUDD *smiles, having picked up on the direction of* BARBARA's *look.*)

JUDD: We seem to have visitors from Mimi's Flamboyant . . .

COLONEL: Well I guess they have nowhere to go. You think there'd be somewhere . . .

(*The* MINISTER *looks up for* WAITER *who appears at once beside him.*)

VAN TRANG: (*In Vietnamese*) The women.

WAITER: (*In Vietnamese*) I'll see to it, sir.

(*The* MINISTER *turns back. Looks at his cards.*)

VAN TRANG: It's a shortage of Americans. With so few GIs left the living is hard. What can they do? You created the industry. Now they're fed up because you're no longer here.

(*The* COLONEL *tries to make light of it.*)

COLONEL: Well I don't know. There are one or two of us . . .

JUDD: Some of us have friends who keep them in work.

(JUDD *smiles. The* MINISTER *ignores this. The women are led*

15

amically away by waiters. BARBARA *still watching.*)

VAN TRANG: One diamond.

COLONEL: A spade.

JUDD: Two hearts.

(*A pause.* BARBARA *is still staring at the women.*)
Barbara?
(*She turns back and, without referring to her cards, shakes her head at the* COLONEL.)

BARBARA: I'm sorry, partner. I'm no help at all.

9. INT. CERCLE SPORTIF. NIGHT

Later. The game is over. The four of them stroll steadily through the now deserted lounge. Behind them you can see their table being cleared. The COLONEL *and* VAN TRANG *are in front, talking quietly together.*

VAN TRANG: Will you be giving us a military briefing?

COLONEL: Certainly. There'll be a situation report. Of course, within the terms of the Paris agreement we can no longer give you military advice.

(*They stroll on.* VAN TRANG *makes no reaction.*)

VAN TRANG: But you have an idea?

COLONEL: I see formations. We think the North will make an offensive in the New Year. It's come to be regular . . . like the baseball season.

(*There is a pause. Then casually*) We'd certainly like to get to see your President Thieu.

(*He steals a quick glance at* VAN TRANG *who does not react.*)
As for the scale of the offensive and where it might come from, it's a little early to say. There are certainly signs of a build-up. Maybe you should look to Tay Ninh.

(*There is a slight pause. The* MINISTER *looks at him. Then turns to the others.*)

VAN TRANG: Thank you, Miss Dean. An excellent evening. Colonel.

COLONEL: Minister.

JUDD: Goodnight.

VAN TRANG: Goodnight.

16

(*He goes. They are by the main entrance.* JUDD *turns casually to* BARBARA.)

JUDD: Barbara, I'll see you home in my car.

BARBARA: I arranged for a cab.

10. EXT. CERCLE SPORTIF. NIGHT

JUDD *and* BARBARA *stand for a moment outside the main entrance to the club. At once there is a giggling noise from the bushes, brief, sharp in the darkness.*

BARBARA: They're still out there.

JUDD: Who?

(*She reaches into her bag for a handful of notes.*)

BARBARA: Will you just take some money across?

(*Before he can answer she anticipates his objections.*)

Would you do it please? As a favour?

JUDD: You know it's not . . .

BARBARA: No. As a favour, Frank?

(FRANK *takes the money reluctantly and goes down the steps.* BARBARA *watches as he crosses the darkened drive and disappears into the bushes. She stands alone in the lit doorway of the Cercle.* FRANK *has now disappeared. Distant voices.*)

WOMAN: Thank you, Number One. You wanna fuck me?

JUDD: No. It's all right. It's a gift.

(*Behind* BARBARA, BOB CHESNEAU *has silently appeared. He is about 28, very intelligent, in beige cotton trousers and a short-sleeved shirt. His speech is always gentle and gracious, like a polite boy. He stands behind* BARBARA, *looking out also.*)

CHESNEAU: Hi.

(*She turns.*)

BARBARA: Hello.

CHESNEAU: You waiting for a taxi?

(BARBARA *smiles in reply.*)

I guess the wheels have finally fallen off.

(*They both smile.*)

If you like I could easily help you. I have a car waiting over there.

(JUDD *has returned, his arm outstretched to* CHESNEAU. *He is bustling with confidence from a mission accomplished.*)

JUDD: Hey, Bob.

CHESNEAU: Frank, how are you?

JUDD: Do you know Barbara?

CHESNEAU: No. No, I don't.

(BARBARA *turns and smiles warmly at* JUDD.)

BARBARA: Bob's kindly offered . . . he's going to run me home.

11. INT. CAR. NIGHT

The car. They are side by side in silence. The half-lit streets of Saigon going by. CHESNEAU *driving.*

BARBARA: Where do you work?

CHESNEAU: I work at the Embassy. I'm a minor official. One of many, I'm afraid.

BARBARA: Why do you drive a Ford Pinto?

(*He smiles.*)

CHESNEAU: Oh I see . . .

BARBARA: I don't understand . . .

CHESNEAU: Neither do we . . .

BARBARA: The allocation. If the CIA is meant to be so secret, why do you all get issued with the same make of car?

CHESNEAU: Beats me. Perhaps a kind of arrogance. And anyway, let's face it, everyone knows. If all the cultural attachés in Saigon were genuine, this would be the most cultured nation on earth.

(*A pause.*)

I'm a spook.

(BARBARA *smiles. She looks out to the streets where the young girls are selling flowers. They hold them out to the cars as they go by.*)

BARBARA: Look . . .

CHESNEAU: Yeah.

BARBARA: They're still out with the jasmine. It's such a beautiful town.

CHESNEAU: Yes it is. I suppose I'd forgotten.

BARBARA: Well, I know. People do.

(*She looks at him. Then away.*)

CHESNEAU: Where do you come from?

BARBARA: Bournemouth. You wouldn't know it. It's the English version of Vung Tau.

CHESNEAU: By the ocean?

BARBARA: Exactly. It's where you go when you're planning to die.

CHESNEAU: Oh yeah? Ours is called Florida.

BARBARA: Yes. Yours has the sun.

12. EXT. APARTMENT BLOCK. NIGHT

The low white apartment block, fronted with palm trees. Chesneau's car stops silently in the deserted street. He gets out of the car to go round and open the car door for her. She gets out. There is a moment's pause, then casually:

BARBARA: Yes. Come up.

(*She goes on ahead.*)

13. INT. APARTMENT. NIGHT

CHESNEAU *sitting forward on a hard chair with a glass of beer in his hands. He is in the middle of the room. His face is lit by a single warm lamp.* BARBARA *sits on the sofa, her legs tucked under her.*

CHESNEAU: It's the ultimate irony really. I joined the CIA to avoid Vietnam. Quite a few of us did the same thing. It was my law professor, he said if you want to avoid a war, the safest place to be is inside the bureaucracy. Tuck yourself away. Join the CIA.

(*A pause.*)

And that was it. They put me in Washington. Strategic analysis, balance of power. I was having a good time. In the way you do. I kept telling myself, well, I don't really work here, I was just avoiding the draft. Till a colleague in the department, as a joke, filled in my name. Like when you order someone *Reader's Digest*, he thought it would be funny if I were sent to Vietnam.

(*He looks across at her.*)

BARBARA: Would you like another beer?

CHESNEAU: Yes, I'll have one more.

(*He watches as she gets up and goes to the big old fridge in the kitchen.*)

You know, I can get you Heineken from the PX.

BARBARA: No really . . .

CHESNEAU: This stuff has probably killed people.

(*She returns with a couple of bottles.*)

BARBARA: I like '33'.

CHESNEAU: You must be tough.

(*She smiles, the old hand. Then settles on the sofa, having given him one.*)

BARBARA: What is your view . . . you must tell me . . . will the South be able to hold on?

CHESNEAU: That is my job. To judge that. That is precisely what I'm doing here.

(*A pause. Then he gets up, putting his beer suddenly to one side.*)

Thank you for the beer. I've enjoyed talking to you.

(*She doesn't move, staring up at him.*)

The days go by. Well, I must thank you.

(*They look at each other a moment. Then he looks at the floor.*)

I hope I'll see you again.

14. INT. APARTMENT. NIGHT

The room seen from the bedroom. BARBARA *sits alone at her desk in her dressing-gown.*

BARBARA: (VO) Dear Mum, I'm sorry it's so long since I've written. To be honest, I've been too busy at work. You'll be pleased with my cheque. A little bit extra. The bank have just come through with my raise.

(*In close-up her hand as she slips the cheque into the already finished letter.*)

(VO) Life here continues very much as usual.

(*Her face, for the first time in close-up, as she licks the envelope.*)

(VO) The Year of the Tiger will soon be the Year of the Cat.

15. INT. BANK. DAY

HENDERSON *standing at one of the metal grilles opposite a shock-haired young Vietnamese,* PHU, *of about 25. He is very angry.*

HENDERSON: I'm sorry. I have to refuse you. It's simply impossible to take all that money out.

    (*He looks sideways at* QUOC *who is at a nearby till.* BARBARA *looks up from her desk.*)

    There are government regulations which expressly forbid the export of large sums.

16. INT. HALIWELL'S OFFICE. DAY

BARBARA *appearing at the door of Haliwell's office.* HALIWELL *is writing at his desk.*

BARBARA: Mr Haliwell . . . I wonder . . . I think Mr Henderson may be needing some assistance out there.

    (QUOC'*s face appears in the doorway behind her, still, serious. But* HALIWELL *carries on writing.*)

HALIWELL: Right. In a moment.

BARBARA: Could you come quickly?

HALIWELL: Yes.

    (*He carries on writing. He does not look up. Quietly, into his work, without moving*) I'm on my way.

17. INT. BANK. DAY

HALIWELL, QUOC *and* BARBARA *moving together like a group of floor-walkers, fast, from a great distance towards the incident.* PHU *takes a small revolver from his pocket.* HENDERSON *is standing opposite.*

PHU: I have a gun.

HENDERSON: Yes.

PHU: I demand my money.

HENDERSON: If you'd like to talk to the manager . . .

    (HALIWELL *steps forward from the group to stand beside* HENDERSON.)

HALIWELL: Mr . . .

HENDERSON: Phu.

HALIWELL: Mr Phu, perhaps I can help you.

21

PHU: I want my money.

HALIWELL: Yes. Yes, of course.

> (*He begins to move across to the grille door between the back and front of the bank.*)

If you'd like to come into my office. . . .

> (*He swings the door open and stands directly opposite* PHU *who is holding the gun.* HALIWELL *looks him straight in the eye.*)

Perhaps I might relieve you of that gun.

18. INT. BANK. DAY

The bank closed. Afternoon. HENDERSON *is laughing, sitting on the edge of Barbara's desk. Way behind him the tellers are locking up their drawers.*

HENDERSON: Well, I must say, you have to hand it to him. Haliwell really came through.

BARBARA: He was lucky.

HENDERSON: It was a tactic. I think we should all be grateful it worked.

> (*He laughs again.* QUOC *comes and sits down near them, quietly resuming his work.*)

To be honest, I was seriously frightened. (*His tone is suddenly intimate.*) You were bloody great.

BARBARA: It worked out well.

> (HENDERSON *smiles a moment, vacantly.*)

HENDERSON: All right, Quoc?

QUOC: Yes thank you, Mr Henderson.

> (*Behind him, a girl who looks to be no more than 14 is getting down from a high stool, picking up her bag, and walking out of frame.*)

One of the tellers has decided to leave.

19. INT. APARTMENT. NIGHT

BARBARA *sitting reading a book. Her legs characteristically tucked up under her. Like a quiet animal. She turns a page, silently. Then looks up.* CHESNEAU *has appeared at the open door to the living room. He carries his jacket and his shirt is marked with sweat.*

CHESNEAU: You should lock the door. I think you're crazy. Do you have any idea of how dangerous it is?

BARBARA: Nobody wants a white English woman.
(*She smiles. She doesn't move from the sofa.*)
How are you?
(*A pause. Then he moves into the room, casually putting a small bunch of flowers down on the table, carelessly, on its side.*)
CHESNEAU: You've not been at the club.
BARBARA: Have you been looking?
(*He nods.*)
No. I've been reading my books. It's wonderful here in the evenings. The silence, lately. The peace.
(*He turns at the window and looks at her.*)
CHESNEAU: I am very emotionally stupid. This is . . . this has always been true. I never know. Even when it's incredibly blatant.
BARBARA: I think this time you probably have the idea.
(*He nods slightly.*)
CHESNEAU: Yeah, I thought I did.
BARBARA: Yes. You have it.
CHESNEAU: Ah. I came round to check.
BARBARA: What a relief . . .
CHESNEAU: Yeah . . .
BARBARA: The embarrassment. If it turned out that you'd got it wrong.
CHESNEAU: Yeah, well, I'd thought of that. . . .
(*He stands, nodding again.*)
It was a factor. Will you have a cigarette?
BARBARA: No. No thanks.
(*He stands a moment, holding the pack out.*)
CHESNEAU: Hey, I was right. Terrific. CIA! Intelligence, huh?

20. INT. APARTMENT. NIGHT
The bed seen from the living room. They are lying together, still. He has his back against the pillows, she is stretched out across him. Her face is on his chest. A single sheet covers the rest of them. We move in as they talk very quietly.
BARBARA: And are you there?
CHESNEAU: No, it's done without me.

23

BARBARA: What, they're . . .

CHESNEAU: They're beaten, then put back in their cells. Today I
went crazy, my best prisoner had been beaten to hell. His
shirt fell open, he had scars . . . welts, right across here . . .
(*He gestures across his own chest.*)

BARBARA: It's wrong.

CHESNEAU: Yeah. But it's also just stupid. He's an important
enemy source.
(*There is a pause.*)
For ten days I've been sitting there. Patiently. A small
wooden table. Just leading him on. I get in today, someone's
got restless, no point in waiting for Chesneau any more. . . .
It's stupid. The agents you capture, they're your life-blood.
You don't go and hit them in the mouth. Hit people in the
mouth, they just go stubborn, or they just tell you what you
most want to hear.
(*He shakes his head.*)
Get the facts first, get things sorted, be sure you've really got
hold of the facts. Then later . . . hell, throw him out of a
helicopter. But afterwards.

BARBARA: Does that happen?
(*He turns and looks at her.*)

CHESNEAU: (*Quietly*) Of course.

21. INT. BATHROOM. NIGHT

Later. BARBARA *is sitting on a small wooden stool, her back against the
wall, with her feet out in front of her on a chair. She is in her
dressing-gown.* CHESNEAU's *face is below her; he is stretched out in the
bath smoking a Marlboro. The only other sound is the occasional
ripple of the water.*

BARBARA: The men at the bank, oh they're quite easygoing. We've
all been here for so long. The Scots are always bankers. Or
else engineers. (*She smiles.*) The funniest is . . . do you know
the British Council?

CHESNEAU: No.

BARBARA: You don't know, but they still have a library here. To
encourage the spread of English culture. Good idea, yes?

24

Here in Saigon?

(*They smile.*)

I went there. There's now just one girl running it. She's Vietnamese. She sits at a desk. I went up to her. She doesn't speak English.

(*They look at each other. They laugh.*)

CHESNEAU: Oh yes. Well, sure.

22. INT. APARTMENT. DAWN

Light beginning to hit the blinds. BARBARA *sitting on the sofa, with* CHESNEAU's *head on her lap, curled up like a child pressed against her breasts. The room held.*

23. INT. BANK. DAY

Morning. BARBARA *in close-up standing waiting at Haliwell's office door as* HALIWELL *arrives for work. A well-defined routine. She is smiling slightly as he goes past her.*

HALIWELL: Good morning, Barbara. How are you?

BARBARA: Fine, Mr Haliwell. Thanks.

(*She starts to unload the pile of ledgers from her arms. He picks up* The Times *from his side of the desk and casually throws it to her.*)

HALIWELL: Look at this. Strikes. Industrial chaos. The whole country seems to be going to hell.

(*She unfolds it with one hand, less than curious.*)

BARBARA: Good Lord.

HALIWELL: I mean, it's national insanity. The unions seem to want to run the whole show. I must say, though, one can count one's blessings.

(*He is hanging up his coat and now turns, smiling.*)

We can all be grateful we're living out here.

24. EXT. OCKHAM'S HOUSE. DAY

The lawn behind Ockham's detached clapboard house. The whole scene gleaming in the sun. There is a party for about fifty people, a mixture of races, all casually dressed. Children are jumping into the portable pool which is next to the house. At the centre a tall,

*intense man in his early fifties, with sunglasses. He is wearing a shirt
and slacks, greeting guests as they arrive. He is* JACK OCKHAM.

OCKHAM: Hi . . . how are you? Nice to see you.

> (CHESNEAU *appears,* BARBARA *a pace behind.*)
> Bob, how are you?

CHESNEAU: This is Barbara Dean. Jack Ockham.

> (OCKHAM *smiles slightly and takes her hand.*)

OCKHAM: I'm very glad you could make it.

CHESNEAU: Barbara works in the bank.

OCKHAM: Good.

> (*He nods slightly.* CHESNEAU *unsure of how to introduce her.*)
> Well, Merry Christmas.

BARBARA: Thank you. And Merry Christmas to you.

> (*Behind them servants are carrying three huge steaming-hot
> turkeys to the white tables which are laid out on the lawn.*
> OCKHAM *passes on to greet the next guests, a short Vietnamese*
> GENERAL *and his taller* WIFE. *They are heard in the background
> as we follow* BARBARA *and* CHESNEAU, *walking into the mass of
> the party.*)
> Are we a couple?

CHESNEAU: What?

BARBARA: In public?

CHESNEAU: I don't know. Do you know?

BARBARA: No.

> (*They both smile.*)
> I enjoy the uncertainty.

CHESNEAU: Yes. Let's not be. For the moment let's stay good
friends.

25. EXT. LAWN. DAY

*Later. A burst of noise and laughter from a table just behind our group
who are* CHESNEAU, BARBARA, FIEDLER, JUDD *and* OCKHAM *who sits
slightly apart.* FIEDLER *has a paper hat. There are streamers and the
debris of a good meal. The atmosphere is easy and slightly drunk.*

OCKHAM: Bob's never understood the aid allocation. You've
never understood it.

CHESNEAU: No, well, that's true.

(COLONEL FIEDLER *explains, for* BARBARA's *benefit.*)

FIEDLER: We want Congress to vote three hundred million dollars to prove they support Thieu's regime.

OCKHAM: Yeah.

FIEDLER: Now in fact . . . three hundred million, well it's not nearly enough, with the economy as bad as it is. We need more than that. But at least it would be symbolic—a symbol of the American intention to help.

(BARBARA *looks across at* CHESNEAU. *He looks down at his hands.*)

Now back home there's a lot of opposition . . .

OCKHAM: Left-wing elements . . .

FIEDLER: Liberals, yeah. People who never liked the war in the first place, who are now saying we should just get out, go home, forget about it. Abandon our friends.

(*He shrugs slightly, as if suppressing the strong feeling he has.*)

Well, I don't think that's a viable option. I don't think that's what Americans should do.

(BARBARA *frowns slightly.*)

BARBARA: But isn't the problem . . .

(*She pauses.*)

CHESNEAU: What?

BARBARA: No, I shouldn't say.

(*There is a pause.* FIEDLER *is looking at* CHESNEAU.)

CHESNEAU: Go on.

BARBARA: No, I really . . . I don't know much about it.

(*She smiles and looks away.*)

OCKHAM: (*With characteristic quiet*) Barbara, you must say what you think.

(*She turns and looks at them.*)

BARBARA: I would have thought the problem you have here is the money will go to a particular regime. A regime whose reputation is for corruption. And there are political prisoners as well . . .

(FIEDLER *easy at the familiarity of this charge.*)

FIEDLER: Oh well, sure, but . . .

BARBARA: Please, I'm not saying . . . for all I know Thieu is the

best man. It's just that if he goes . . . you will go with him.
You may be sitting on a branch that's withered. That's all.
(*A pause.* CHESNEAU *is looking at her.*)

FIEDLER: Well, I don't think . . .

BARBARA: It's . . .

FIEDLER: There's no sign of that. The regime is hardly
threatened from within.

BARBARA: No?
(*He is staring at her, frowning.*)

FIEDLER: Barbara, there's only one enemy. That's the enemy
that's waiting out there.

26. EXT. LAWN. NIGHT

*At once, the whole scene seen from the bushes, far away and at
night. There is now a barbecue around which people are gathered
and others are jumping into the darkened pool. Raised voices and
laughter. It is eerie. The shot held.*

27. EXT. HOUSE. NIGHT

BARBARA *and* CHESNEAU *left sitting alone on the now deserted lawn,
as the party continues indoors. Distant whooping around a lit tree
indoors.*

CHESNEAU: I decided . . . while you were talking, watching you
arguing it out . . . I thought tomorrow I'm going to go in
there. It's time I told everyone what I really think.
(BARBARA *is watching him closely.*)
We're so obsessed with this aid allocation that we pretend
that things are much worse than they are. We think that
only by exaggerating are we going to get all the money we
need. (*He shakes his head.*) All the time we're saying, it's
coming, it's coming, quick, give us money, give us aid. But
that battle back there in Washington has become more real
to us than anything here.
(*There is a particularly loud whoop from the house, as of a
violent party game.*)

BARBARA: I must say, from the way they're behaving . . . it
doesn't look as if they really think it's the end.

CHESNEAU: No, of course not. Charades.
(*He pauses, then moves his glass away.*)
But meanwhile the facts get pushed out the way.

28. INT. APARTMENT. NIGHT
The apartment still at night. BARBARA *in bed. The sound of a very distant explosion, a rumble in the night.* CHESNEAU *is seen to be standing at the window, with a towel wrapped round his middle.*
BARBARA: What is it?
CHESNEAU: Oh it's the gas dump. It's always the gas dump when it's that close.
(*He holds the blind apart, staring out absently.*)
They pretend. They send up rockets. But really the job is done from the inside.
BARBARA: What d'you mean?
CHESNEAU: Well, they always put up the firecrackers. . . .
(*He smiles and makes an arc with his arm.*)
Great lights in the night. So you think it's being bombed. But in fact there's always an employee working for the VC on the inside, all he's done is slip a detonator in.
(*He turns and looks at her. The noise has died.*)
All the rest is show. They like to do it. I don't know why.
BARBARA: Perhaps because subversion's too easy.
(*He looks across at her.*)
CHESNEAU: Something like that.

29. INT. APARTMENT. NIGHT
BARBARA *in her white dressing-gown sitting directly across from* CHESNEAU *at a small table. He is still in his towel. They are sipping tea from small Chinese cups, in the middle of the night.*
CHESNEAU: Can you give me an idea of England?
BARBARA: Well. . . . (*She smiles.*) The place is very wet. Which makes its greenness almost iridescent. It is almost indecently green.
(*They smile.*)
The people are—odd. They're cruel to each other. Mostly

in silent . . . in unexpected ways. It's an emotional cruelty. You feel watched, disapproved of all the time.

CHESNEAU: That's why you got away?

BARBARA: There's a terrible pressure, all these little hedgerows squeezing you in, tight little lines of upright houses. Everyone spying on everyone else.

(*She looks over at him and smiles.*)

I'm not even . . . an unconventional woman. I need only that amount of air. But I can't get it in England.

(*There is a pause.* CHESNEAU *is looking at her.*)

I know what you're thinking. Will I ever go back?

30. INT. BANK. DAY

The hustle of the bank at lunchtime. Shafts of sunlight falling as in a cathedral across the back area, while at the front it is very busy before lunch. BARBARA *is at her desk, staring hopelessly at a sheaf of papers.* QUOC *comes over to wait for her verdict.*

BARBARA: Quoc, I'm afraid this isn't possible. Really there's no question of this.

(*She looks up at him regretfully.*)

It's pointless investing money in transport now the Vietcong are blowing up roads.

QUOC: Shall I say this to him?

BARBARA: Yes. If you want to. I mean . . . yes. It's impossible. How can I possibly defend an investment when we're approaching the worst time of year? I mean of course, yes, when the rains come, I'll consider it again. But until the rains . . . there is uncertainty. Can you tell him?

QUOC: Yes. As you say.

(HENDERSON *has appeared at the desk, hovering. His shirt is cleaner, his beard trimmer than ever.* QUOC *is putting more papers on Barbara's desk.*)

That. Just a signature.

BARBARA: Hello, Donald.

HENDERSON: I wonder, could I have a word?

BARBARA: Yes of course. What can I do for you?

QUOC: (*Discreetly*) And another signature there.

(HENDERSON *waits for* QUOC *to finish.* BARBARA *speaks
meanwhile.*)

BARBARA: Tell Mr Haliwell about these decisions. If you want
my judgement checked against his . . .

QUOC: No, it isn't necessary.
(*He takes the papers and goes.* BARBARA *sighs.*)

BARBARA: Oh Lord, do you think it's a personal friend?
(HENDERSON *shrugs slightly.*)

HENDERSON: My point is this. I need to ask you. . . .
(*He pauses, uncomfortable.*)
Do you think I'll ever be promoted in here?

BARBARA: What are you saying?
(*She looks at him, levelly.*)
You mean you're leaving?

HENDERSON: Yes, well, possibly. I'm not really sure.
(*He looks down, embarrassed.*)
I mean, there's you and above you there's Haliwell. Neither
of you seem as if you're likely to retire. So the fact is . . . I
got round to thinking . . . well, I've been offered a job in
Hong Kong.

BARBARA: Good. You must take it.

HENDERSON: Yes. I would like to. That's right.
(*They stare at each other.*)

BARBARA: Well, that's nice. We'll arrange a party.
(*He looks at her, then suddenly bursts, like an overflowing
sink.*)

HENDERSON: You know, I am most terribly in love.
(*She looks panic-stricken round the bank.*)

BARBARA: Yes, well, I think this is . . .

HENDERSON: Honestly.

BARBARA: Hardly the moment . . .

HENDERSON: Just the thought I might not see you again . . .
(BARBARA *turns relieved to* QUOC *who has returned with more
papers.*)

BARBARA: Yes?
(HENDERSON *suddenly shouts at the top of his voice.*)

HENDERSON: Oh God, Quoc, will you never ever leave us? Can't

31

we have one moment on our own?
(*There is a pause. All over the bank people stop work and look up.* QUOC *is shocked, but looks impassively at* HENDERSON.)

QUOC: I'm sorry.

BARBARA: No . . . You must stay here. Mr Henderson is just a little upset.
(*She looks up at* HENDERSON, *quietly furious*.)

HENDERSON: Yes. God, I'm sorry.

BARBARA: He doesn't mean it. He had no intention of being so rude.
(HENDERSON *shakes his head weakly*.)

HENDERSON: Really I'm sorry, it's unforgivable . . .
(QUOC *looks at them, nods*.)

QUOC: In a few moments, I shall return.

31. INT. BANK. EVENING
The bank, dark now. Among the empty desks HENDERSON *sits with his head in his hands.* BARBARA *is leaning against a desk nearby. Beyond them in the distance a young Vietnamese girl with a long pole closes the shutters on the high windows.*

HENDERSON: Oh my God, Barbara, I can tell you despise me.

BARBARA: Have I said anything?

HENDERSON: No. Not at all. It's just . . . your general demeanour. You behave as if I'm doing something wrong.
(BARBARA *looks down at him, as if a little surprised*.)
I do have to tell you, I've been going crazy . . .

BARBARA: Well, in that case it's best that you leave. Hong Kong is a good place to forget me. (*She smiles slightly, amused at the ludicrousness of the remark*.) So you'll be much happier there.
(*She is looking at the floor*.)

HENDERSON: I would like . . . I feel you disapprove of me.
(*She does not answer*.)
You feel I'm cowardly, that's right? (BARBARA *smiles, this time bitterly, at the inadequacy of what she will say*.)

32

BARBARA: I think that we . . . who were not born here . . .
   should make sure we go with dignity.
   (*There is a pause.*)
   That's all.

32. INT. BANK. DAY
Morning. The bank is busy again. Tellers moving back and forth. In the middle of the back area, HENDERSON, *turned away from us, is clearing out his desk, like an expelled pupil, as the commerce of the bank goes on.*
BARBARA: (VO) Donald *did* leave with comparative dignity.
   (BARBARA *watches him, from behind her desk.*)
   Compared with some of the rest of us, I mean.
   (*She turns. Her eye catches camera.*)

PART TWO

33. INT. CAR. DAY

Fade-up inside the car. CHESNEAU's *face as he drives through early-morning Saigon. There is a cigarette hanging from his mouth. The cool morning goes by outside. The image holds. Then after a few seconds . . .*

BARBARA: (VO) I used to see Bob whenever it was possible. When we could we met, discreetly, in my room. As time went by it became much harder. . . .

34. EXT. EMBASSY. DAY

The great white bulk of the American Embassy in Saigon, cut out against the morning sky. Palm trees and lawns in front of the huge square building. The gates open, the barrier goes up, CHESNEAU's *Pinto goes through, with a greeting from the guard.*

BARBARA: (VO) He could only manage an occasional hour. Anyone who worked in that great white building seemed to vanish inside for the day. . . .

35. INT. EMBASSY LOBBY. DAY

CHESNEAU *crossing the guarded lobby of the Embassy, carrying a briefcase. He makes for the elevator, showing his pass as he goes.*

BARBARA: (VO) It was a city inside a city. Always, it seemed, with a life of its own.
(*The elevator doors close.*)

36. INT. CORRIDOR. DAY

CHESNEAU *walks along the long neon-lit corridor at the spine of* CIA

*headquarters on the fifth floor of the Embassy. A jump in
sound: typewriters, telexes, shredders, people calling from room to
room.*

BARBARA: (VO) On the fifth floor of the Embassy, the New Year
  had begun much as they'd expected. Offensives from the
  North had started on time. . . .
  (*Lines of doors on either side, through which we see desk
  workers, strategic analysts. The maps, the desks, the charts, the
  projections, the files. Piles and piles of paperwork. Everyone is
  in civilian clothing.*)
  (VO) The town of Phuoc Binh fell at the beginning of
  January.
  (*A cry of* 'Hi, Bob' *from one of the doors.*)
  (VO) But then Ban me Thuot followed early in March.

37. INT. OFFICE. DAY
CHESNEAU *standing with his secretary* LINDA *in the communal
secretaries' office. She is 24, blonde, big-jawed and plaid-skirted, in
the Mid-Western way. He is nodding at some papers she is showing
him.*

BARBARA: (VO) Somehow up till then nothing really told them
  this was going to be the long-awaited end. . . .
  (CHESNEAU *nods as the* SECRETARY *explains a document to
  him.*)
  (VO) They'd lived through so many of these annual
  readjustments, at first they'd just assumed it was another of
  the same. . . .

38. INT. CORRIDOR. DAY
CHESNEAU *walking on, purposefully, down the corridor towards the
far end.*

BARBARA: (VO) Of course, I suppose if they'd just looked around
  them, if they'd ever just stopped and thought. . . .
  (CHESNEAU *reaches the end room. The door is open. Ockham's
  office. There are ten people sitting round in the deep-blue
  carpeted office, with a pine desk where* OCKHAM *is.* CHESNEAU
  stops at the open door.)

35

(VO) But somehow . . . all of us . . . our eye was elsewhere.

(OCKHAM *looks up from behind his desk.*)

(VO) When we realized, it was too late.

39. INT. OFFICE. DAY

At once we join the scene which has plainly already been long in progress. A young OFFICER *lectures from a wall map of Vietnam, pointing with a short stick. Sitting round in the other chairs we see* COLONEL FIEDLER *and* JUDD, *among a mixture of analysts and military.* OCKHAM *is standing staring ahead, a picture of President Ford behind him.* CHESNEAU *sits down, as we pick up the* OFFICER *in mid-brief.*

OFFICER: . . . hemmed in on the road. The South has lost fifteen hamlets in twenty-four hours. Here. On the road between Quang Tri and Hue. (*He points further down the map.*) Two district towns gone here in Quang Tin. The North heading down towards Tam Ky. (*Further down.*) Ban me Thuot here, of course, consolidated. And the anticipated push to Tay Ninh. . . . (*He points.*) Signs of that are finally happening. This morning they lost the town of Tri Tam. (*He stands a moment, almost apologetic.*)

FIEDLER: Jesus Christ, they're coming out everywhere . . .

OCKHAM: No, it's not so. . . .

(*He nods at the* OFFICER *to sit down.*)

It's logical, I'm afraid. Once President Thieu decided to abandon the Highlands, everything that's happened makes logical sense.

(*There is a pause.*)

FIEDLER: Do we know more?

OCKHAM: Joan . . .

(OCKHAM, *anticipating, has already nodded at* JOAN MACKINTOSH, *who has got up. She is a CIA analyst, a brisk, well-built woman of about 40, in a pleated summer dress. She goes over to the map.*)

MACKINTOSH: We have this from Thieu's Cabinet.

(FIEDLER *looks at* OCKHAM, *surprised.*)

OCKHAM: We now have an agent in there.

MACKINTOSH: He explains. He says there is a new strategy. (*With a cloth she wipes the old marks from the laminated map.*) I'm afraid it was only invented this week.

(*She takes a pentel and draws a thick line horizontally across South Vietnam from just above Tay Ninh to Nha Trang, so that the country is neatly divided three-quarters of the way down.*)

That . . . a defensive line. . . .

(*Then she draws three tiny semicircles, way up on the coast in the North, all isolated from the main defensive area. They are around Quang-Nai, Tam-Ky, and Hue and Danang.*)

Here . . . these enclaves . . . these coastal towns. . . . (*She turns back.*) Nothing else. The rest is abandoned.

FIEDLER: (*Quietly*) My God.

MACKINTOSH: (*As quietly*) There we are.

(*There is a silence. As if to fill it, apologetically, in contrast to her earlier manner, MACKINTOSH explains.*) It isn't . . . we don't think it would be a bad strategy. It's always been an option the South has had. What is disastrous is simply the speed of it. It was intended this option should cover six months. Instead of which it's been three days now since it was implemented and of course . . . (*She looks to OCKHAM, as if deferring to him, tying herself up slightly as she finishes.*) . . . to do with its suddenness, I think . . . now it's happening, well, we all know . . . it does seem as if it's panic all round.

(*There is a long pause. OCKHAM stares ahead. From the back CHESNEAU speaks quietly.*)

CHESNEAU: Where's the Ambassador?

(OCKHAM *doesn't answer at once.*)

Still getting his teeth fixed?

OCKHAM: I have it here.

(*He nods and reaches among the pile of telexes on his desk. He reads from the appropriate wire.*)

Minor orthodontal surgery was completed in North Carolina last week.

37

CHESNEAU: And is he coming back?

OCKHAM: Yeah. Eventually. (*He reads from the cable again.*) He says 'No panic.' That's it. 'The situation is not yet serious.' (*He drops it on the desk, then quietly*) I think that maybe we'd better leave it there.

(*He nods to dismiss them. People rise uncertainly,* CHESNEAU *looking at* JUDD. OCKHAM *at once starts to talk to* FIEDLER.)

Thank you, everyone. Colonel, if you got a moment . . .

(*But we go with* CHESNEAU *and* JUDD, *leaving together in a group of agents, talking under their breath.*)

CHESNEAU: It's Loonyville. Land of the Loonies!

JUDD: That's right.

40. INT. CORRIDOR. DAY

Continuous. As they come out into the corridor and are able to raise their voices, the hysteria begins to seep.

CHESNEAU: Oh my God, the spooks are going *crazy*.

(*People around them scatter, still talking, as they go on down the corridor,* JUDD *already tapping satirically at his teeth with his fingernail and smiling.*)

JUDD: Teeth!

CHESNEAU: Yeah.

JUDD: What's he going to do with them? Bite the fucking VC in the neck?

(*They go on down the corridor. Suddenly the remains of the meeting has broken up and all the other agents and officers have disappeared, leaving* JUDD *and* CHESNEAU *the last two.*

CHESNEAU *puts his hand on* JUDD's *arm as they disappear.*)

CHESNEAU: Frank. Suppose it happens. And we evacuate. . . .

(*They disappear. The deserted corridor. We catch* CHESNEAU's *voice from round the corner.*)

Has anyone thought to look at the plans?

(*A pause. We look at the empty corridor.*)

41. EXT. WASTEGROUND. NIGHT

CHESNEAU's *Pinto silently drawing up on a piece of wrecked Saigon suburb. It is so quiet it is as if he has turned the engine off. He comes*

*to a halt. There is just open ground, with some shacks away in
the distance, and alone in the wasteground a small tin garage.*
CHESNEAU *lights a cigarette. He sits a moment in the car. Then he
gets out and begins to walk across the silent wasteground.*

42. INT. GARAGE. NIGHT
CHESNEAU *opening the corrugated-iron door. The night seen briefly
behind him as he slips in. The door closes. At the end a man is
sitting on a crate, behind some tyres. He is 40, thin, with
exceptionally bad skin. He wears sun-glasses. His name is* NHIEU.
CHESNEAU *speaks quietly.*
CHESNEAU: Hi. How are you?
NHIEU: I am well, thank you.
CHESNEAU: That's good.
NHIEU: I want this to be our final meeting. I don't want
     money. I want documents out.
     (CHESNEAU *stands still at the door.*)
CHESNEAU: Well, if you like. It may not be necessary. I don't
     think anyone knows what you do.
NHIEU: It is a condition.
     (CHESNEAU *nods slightly, in assent.*)
     When?
CHESNEAU: Your papers? Soon.
NHIEU: Tomorrow. And traveller's cheques. American
     Express.
     (NHIEU'*s voice is firm. There is a slight pause.*)
CHESNEAU: Please tell me first what you have from Hanoi.
NHIEU: There was a Cabinet meeting last night. It is now the
     intention of the Government of the North to press the
     war as far as it will go.
CHESNEAU: Yes, but is it . . .?
NHIEU: It will be military.
CHESNEAU: What makes you say that?
NHIEU: They call it blood scent. (*He gestures to his nose.*) The
     smell of blood in their noses. They will fight, all the way
     to Saigon.
     (CHESNEAU *is seen to weigh this up, then decide to go on.*)

39

CHESNEAU: You see, the thought was they might stop short of the city . . .

(NHIEU *shakes his head at once*.)

NHIEU: No.

CHESNEAU: And negotiate for a coalition from strength.

NHIEU: Up till last night, yes, there was a faction. But they are defeated. They will fight their way in.

(CHESNEAU *looks at him, then goes on*.)

CHESNEAU: This time, I'm sorry, I will have to ask you how close the source is.

NHIEU: Has he ever been wrong?

(NHIEU *looks straight at him, holding his stare*.)

CHESNEAU: When?

NHIEU: Three weeks. The end of April. (*He smiles slightly*.) I am not staying. I will be gone.

43. EXT. WASTEGROUND. NIGHT

The two men pacing together slowly back across the ground. They look small against the vastness of the night, and the tone is of two elder statesmen.

NHIEU: I have a cousin in Omaha, Nebraska.

CHESNEAU: Ah.

NHIEU: He has a business selling paint.

CHESNEAU: Ah yes. (*He steals a quick glance at him*.) It's very quiet in Nebraska.

NHIEU: You are saying I will find no business as a pimp?

(CHESNEAU *shrugs slightly*.)

CHESNEAU: Well, I don't know. It's a land of opportunity.

NHIEU: I was hoping also, I might take some girls?

(*They stop*, CHESNEAU *registering the request, but not reacting. They have reached the car*.)

CHESNEAU: I will try.

(*He is about to get in*.)

Thank you. You've been a great help to us.

NHIEU: The documents.

CHESNEAU: Yes. I will see it's arranged.

44. INT. OFFICES. NIGHT

The deserted CIA offices at dead of night. The secretaries' shared office is completely quiet, and through the open door we see CHESNEAU *at work by a single lamp.*

He reaches for a clean yellow legal pad, and quickly writes a few Vietnamese names on it. Then he pulls open a drawer in the side of his desk and takes out a fat, black address book. He opens it. It is thick, bulging, messy. Years of writing in both English and Vietnamese. He flicks a couple of times over some pages, then starts systematically transferring names from the book to his pad. Crossfade to:

45. INT. OFFICE. DAWN

CHESNEAU *sitting back at his desk, the work complete in front of him, the morning light coming through the blinds. There's a pause. Then he gets up and picks up the list, walks off down the corridor.*

46. INT. OCKHAM'S OFFICE. DAY

OCKHAM *is already at his desk, in shirt-sleeves. He has a cup of coffee at his side, and he is sitting reading the day's telexes with his legs up on the table.* CHESNEAU *comes in quietly at the door.*

CHESNEAU: Jack, you're in. (*He nods at a few sheets of paper he has left on the desk top.*) I left that for you.

OCKHAM: Yeah, I got it.

CHESNEAU: Did you take a look?

> (OCKHAM *nods slightly.*)
>
> I've been making a list. (*He approaches the desk with his yellow legal pad.*) Here's a list of our two hundred most important local contacts. They should be the first we take out. (*He settles down to explain.*) I think the way we do it is, each department draws up a list of its most sensitive men . . .

OCKHAM: Bob, I don't disagree with you. But the Ambassador has to say when. (*He goes on before* CHESNEAU *can interrupt.*) I've already called him. He arrived back in the country last night. (CHESNEAU *is looking at him, mistrustfully.*)

CHESNEAU: Jack, these are the people who've actively worked for us . . .

OCKHAM: Sure.

CHESNEAU: There's a whole dependent community here. Don't say if the Communists finally get here, we're just going to leave them to be murdered in their beds.

OCKHAM: No question of that. We take them with us. (*He pauses, as calm as ever.*) The question is one of time-scale, that's all.

CHESNEAU: Well, in three weeks . . .

OCKHAM: You don't have to argue. At least you don't have to argue with me.

(*He smiles slightly, and looks across at* CHESNEAU.)

The Ambassador's read the report of your agent. He's insisting he sees you himself.

47. INT. AMBASSADOR'S OFFICE. DAY

The Ambassador's office is lined in dark wood. It has a deep-green carpet and fine desk, with flags behind it and photographs of the Ambassador with successive Presidents—Johnson, Nixon, Ford. The AMBASSADOR *is a very tall man in his early sixties in a tropical suit. He is sandy-haired, with a disconcerting habit of sometimes seeming neither to see you nor hear you. He gets up as soon as* CHESNEAU *and* OCKHAM *come into the room, making low murmurs as he settles them in chairs.*

OCKHAM: Ambassador.

AMBASSADOR: Hi. Good morning. (*He gestures towards a chair.*) Why don't you sit down?

(*As they settle, the* AMBASSADOR *wanders, making vague noises.*)

Bob . . . OK . . . Jack, how you doing?

(*Then he settles at his own desk.*)

Right. Here we are then. . . . (*He looks at* CHESNEAU.) I read your report. I have to tell you . . . I don't admire it. This is not the sort of thing I like to read. This war has always been a great test of character . . . at this time more than ever perhaps. (*He now gestures at the report on the desk.*) This simply contradicts all our information. This 'blood scent' theory . . .

CHESNEAU: Yeah.

(*The* AMBASSADOR *stops, waiting for* CHESNEAU *to say more.*)

The agent is good.

AMBASSADOR: I'm afraid I simply don't accept that. Nothing he says squares with the picture we have. I have read it. Thank you for submitting it. But I shall not credit it when making policy.

(*He smiles at* OCKHAM.)

OCKHAM: I think that's right.

AMBASSADOR: I'm telling Washington the North are still keen to negotiate . . .

(*The* AMBASSADOR *has sat back now, and is off on his own tack.*) This latest round of fighting has been very bracing. It's led to some decisions which were long overdue. President Thieu has succeeded in stripping down the country, he's made it a much more defensible shape. The area we're left with is much more logical, that's the benefit of strategic withdrawal. Now when we fight we're in the right positions. As soon as they see that, the Communists will stop. That's the moment we'll be able to negotiate . . .

CHESNEAU: Sir, I don't think it'll happen like that.

(*There is a pause. The* AMBASSADOR *smiles easily.*)

AMBASSADOR: Well, it won't happen if everyone panics . . . if everyone starts spreading depression and alarm . . .

CHESNEAU: No, it's just. . . .

(*He looks for support to* OCKHAM, *who gives none.*) Our reports from the military indicate a chronic problem of morale.

(*The* AMBASSADOR *shifts slightly in his chair.*)

AMBASSADOR: I wonder sometimes if we don't project that. I mean, if the problem isn't more in ourselves. Because we ourselves are a little bit panicky. . . . (*He pauses, hanging the sentence in the air.*) So then we kind of see it in the Vietnamese.

(CHESNEAU *starts again, calmly, trying to keep to the facts.*)

CHESNEAU: Sir, I'm worried we corrupt our intelligence. All last year we said things were bad. That was to dramatize, to secure an aid allocation. Now you're asking us to say things are good.

AMBASSADOR: Yes well, God, man, I still need money . . .

CHESNEAU: What?

AMBASSADOR: That's exactly why your stuff has got to be suppressed. (*He gestures angrily at* CHESNEAU'*s report.*) Congress is hardly going to vote us more money if they believe that South Vietnam's about to be destroyed.

CHESNEAU: So you're . . .

(*But the* AMBASSADOR *has suddenly started raising his voice.*)

AMBASSADOR: And it's *not* going to be! God, how often do I have to say? (*He suddenly starts shouting, with hurt and bewilderment.*) What is this in us? Some kind of *death wish*? Some kind of wishing the whole thing would end?

(*There is a pause.*)

CHESNEAU: (*As tactfully as he can*) I think our first duty is to anyone who helped us. It's our job to get those people out . . .

AMBASSADOR: Out of the question. No evacuation. I'm not doing anything that smells of defeat.

CHESNEAU: Sir, I can promise it won't be conspicuous . . .

AMBASSADOR: Oh yes, that's fine. What? Planes overhead? (*He makes an angry gesture to the sky.*) Great lines at Tan Son Nhut airport? Oh my God, yes, we really need that.

(CHESNEAU *interrupts before he finishes.*)

CHESNEAU: No, I am saying . . . some of the Vietnamese commanders, the men who are out in the field right now, the reason they are fighting so badly is because we've made no plans for their families and friends. Now if we could get that worry removed for them . . .

(*The* AMBASSADOR *turns to* OCKHAM.)

AMBASSADOR: He's saying he would like us to prepare for defeat.

(CHESNEAU *insists at once.*)

CHESNEAU: No, I'm not.

AMBASSADOR: There would be chaos.

CHESNEAU: There'll be even greater chaos if we delay. If we leave it to the very last minute, can you imagine what that's going to be like?

(*There is a pause. The* AMBASSADOR *looks at him.*)

AMBASSADOR: Chesneau, my aim is exactly to avoid that.
There will be no last minute here.

CHESNEAU: Sir . . .

AMBASSADOR: The North will stop short and I will negotiate. But it's essential I do that from strength.

(CHESNEAU *is about to interrupt again.*)

That is why I need a new aid allocation. I've asked for seven hundred million this week. The President has promised he will get it from Congress. (*He sits back.*) Until then we are going to sit tight.

CHESNEAU: (*Very quiet now*) But sir . . . with respect . . . you didn't get it last time. In effect you're gambling with thousands of lives.

AMBASSADOR: We are going to prove our absolute friendship.

CHESNEAU: Even if it costs our friends their own lives?

(*There is a pause. The debate is over. The* AMBASSADOR *speaks, full of sorrow.*)

AMBASSADOR: Bob. I don't like to see you hysterical. I know the work has gotten very hard. I don't like to see you join the conspiracy. (*He looks up at him a moment.*) You of all people.

(*His own melancholy is so apparent that* CHESNEAU *cannot reply.*)

Well . . . there we are.

(OCKHAM *looks up, shifting as if the meeting is over. But the* AMBASSADOR *has turned into himself and is staring at his desk.*)

OCKHAM: Well . . .

(*The* AMBASSADOR *looks up.*)

AMBASSADOR: I lost a son.

CHESNEAU: Yes. I'm sorry, sir.

AMBASSADOR: My son was killed fighting. He died here. Six years ago. (*He looks at* CHESNEAU.) No, well, Bob, thanks for the offer. But I don't think we'll be leaving right now.

48. INT. APARTMENT. NIGHT

Darkness. Then BARBARA's *face, just hit with a streak of light as she unlatches the door.* CHESNEAU *is standing outside on the landing.*

45

CHESNEAU: Hi, how are you?

(*He smiles. She looks at him a moment.*)

I wanted to see you.

(*She opens the door.*)

BARBARA: Come in. The curfew . . .

CHESNEAU: Oh it's all right.

(*She closes the door behind him and goes on past him back into the apartment which is darkened, unlit.*)

I'm afraid I've been drinking. One or two of the Agency. . . .

(*He stands a moment at the door, apologetically, holding a couple of bottles in his hand. She has gone to sit down at the far end of the apartment on a wooden chair.*)

Have you been sleeping?

BARBARA: I'm sitting in the dark.

(*There is a pause. He moves into the darkened room.*)

CHESNEAU: It's been very bad. Things are bad lately. There's an airlift out of Danang. Hue gone, Danang going . . .

BARBARA: I heard the World Service tonight.

(*He stands a moment. She is not looking at him.*)

CHESNEAU: Listen, I'm sorry . . . I've not been coming to see you. I'm sure . . . you must be angry, I know. It's just . . . it gets to be impossible . . .

BARBARA: Why do you behave as if I'm your wife?

CHESNEAU: What?

BARBARA: (*Quietly, with no apparent bitterness*) It's unattractive. Pouring out excuses. 'I'm sorry, darling, I'm drunk. . . .' I'm your girlfriend, there's no responsibility. And thank goodness, no need to report.

(CHESNEAU *looks at her a moment, not understanding her mood.*)

CHESNEAU: Barbara, I'm sorry, I felt you'd be angry . . .

BARBARA: Yes, well, I am. Things are coming to an end. That means going into work hasn't been easy. It's not very pleasant, the look people have. Today there was a girl, a teller, she's been working at the bank, I suppose, two years, she came to me to ask if I could help get her out. I said,

46

well, there's a friend of mine. . . (*She looks at him quickly, then away.*) . . . he can get papers, I think.

CHESNEAU: Yeah, it's not . . . it isn't too easy. For the moment we're playing things down.
(*He pauses, miserably.* BARBARA *is looking down at her hands.*)
I mean, of course I will for a friend of yours, Barbara. We're trying to not to let panic set in.
(*He goes on, apologetically. She doesn't turn.*)
That's why the radio doesn't quite come through with things. All the news of the military defeats. We don't want things to get too conspicuous. People might take to the streets.

BARBARA: Well, I'm sure. You must lie to them. Lying's got you this far.

CHESNEAU: Barbara, you know I have always protested . . .

BARBARA: Yes of course. . . . (*She turns to him at last.*) You've protested to *me*.
(*There is a pause.*)
I remember you so many evenings, lying there. A chance to talk about your work. Then you've gone back into the Embassy . . .

CHESNEAU: Barbara . . .

BARBARA: *Done nothing.* And now you're inventing a fresh set of lies. (*She turns away.*) 'Oh whatever we do we mustn't tell the people. Just get the palefaces out of this mess. . . .'

CHESNEAU: That isn't fair. That's not fair to us. The whole thing is just . . . to keep things in hand.
(*There is a miserable silence.*)

BARBARA: (*Very quietly.*) This girl said to me, 'I know you'll betray us.' I said, 'Oh I don't think that's true.' She said, 'Oh please you mustn't be offended . . .' (*She turns and looks at him.*) '. . . I know what you do is always for the best.'
(*She gets up and goes out of the room. In the distance a light comes on and she passes out of sight.* CHESNEAU *alone in the room holding his beer. Then* BARBARA's *voice calling through.*)
These people *know*. They know what's happening. The

more you lie, the worse it will get.
(CHESNEAU *turns slightly.*)
CHESNEAU: We don't know for sure that everything's over.
(BARBARA's *face reappears in the doorway.*)
BARBARA: In that case you're the only people who don't.

49. INT. CORRIDOR. DAY

The main corridor in the CIA. Empty. The noise of people at work in the offices. Then after a few seconds the most almighty explosion not far away. The whole corridor shakes. At once people come running, JUDD *first.*
JUDD: Jesus Christ, what the hell is happening?

50. INT. UPSTAIRS CORRIDOR. DAY

The AMBASSADOR *appears, hands on hips, furious in the deserted corridor upstairs.*
AMBASSADOR: What the hell is going on here?

51. INT. STAIRWELL. DAY

The enormous stairwell at the centre of the Embassy. The AMBASSADOR *appears on the stairs. Above him, a door is opened at the very top of the well, and an anxious American* MARINE *is seen staring up into the sky. The* AMBASSADOR *yells up from the railing three floors below.*
AMBASSADOR: Soldier, what's happening?
(*The* MARINE *calls back down.*)
MARINE: There's just one fighter, sir. He's bombing the
Presidential Palace, it's like.
(*A very loud voice through the whole building, screaming at full pitch.*)
VOICE: Hey. Get away from the windows. *Everyone.* Get down
on the floor.

52. INT. CORRIDOR. DAY

The corridor now with forty people lying dead-still on the ground, as for a post-nuclear exercise. A pause. Then the whine of an approaching jet and another tremendous explosion. The corridor

*shakes again. Then the sound of the jet disappearing into the
distance. Silence. Nobody moves.
Then the first person sits up.*

53. INT. OCKHAM'S OFFICE. DAY
*A couple of minutes later. A jump in sound as from outside you
can hear people sorting themselves out, calling to one another, as
CHESNEAU comes into the room. OCKHAM is already on the phone
at his desk, apparently as calm as ever.*

OCKHAM: (*Phone.*) OK. All right.

CHESNEAU: What the hell was that about?
  (OCKHAM *looks up briefly.*)

OCKHAM: (*Phone.*) OK. Yeah. I understand.

CHESNEAU: Jack.
  (OCKHAM *nods and puts down the phone.*)

OCKHAM: Some mad pilot. A cowboy. Decided to fight the
  war on his own.
  (*He shrugs slightly and turns back to his desk to sit down.*
  JUDD *has come in to join them.*)
  What can you do? There's very little damage . . .

CHESNEAU: Nobody knew what the hell was happening. (*He
  has begun to shout.*) Nobody had any idea how to deal
  with it.

OCKHAM: No, well, of course.
  (*He looks at him, very quiet, his calm for the first time
  seeming unnatural, almost pathological.*)
  It was a surprise.
  (*He reaches for a bottle of whisky from a drawer in his desk.*
  CHESNEAU *looks at him, rattled by his elaborate calm.*)

CHESNEAU: Jack, I thought we had radar defences. This town
  is meant to be ringed. That maniac came clear through
  the airspace . . .

OCKHAM: Yes, I know.

CHESNEAU: We're just sitting here. (*He looks up to the ceiling.*)
  When is that mad bastard in that office going to realize
  we need to get out?
  (*A pause.* OCKHAM *looks at* JUDD, *who is looking at the floor.*)

OCKHAM: Bob, understand you have my permission. If you're unhappy, you're free to resign.

54. EXT. BASEBALL GROUND. DAY
CHESNEAU *stands in the bleachers watching the lunchtime baseball in the Embassy compound.* JUDD *has followed him out.*
CHESNEAU: It's not even me, it's not me I'm thinking of . . .
JUDD: No . . .
CHESNEAU: I don't give a shit what happens to us.
(*He sits down on one of the benches and gets out a sandwich.* JUDD *sits beside him.*)
It's those thousands of people who helped us. We made them a promise. And it's getting too late. The Ambassador dreams of some personal triumph. Ockham moves his furniture out . . .
JUDD: I didn't know that.
CHESNEAU: Sure. *Things.* Joan's cat. . . .
(*He nods at* JOAN *who is approaching them.*)
Objects. Money. Everything but the *people* can go.
(JOAN *opens her handbag to give a note to* JUDD. *Inside* CHESNEAU *sees a .45 pistol.*)
New gun, Joan?
MACKINTOSH: I got it in case we ever get caught.
(*She smiles at* JUDD.)
Frank and I . . . we have an agreement. We're going to shoot each other in the head.
(*She goes.* CHESNEAU *watches her leave, but* JUDD *has turned and is looking at* CHESNEAU, *as if preparing to say something difficult.*)
JUDD: Bob, I've been wanting to say to you, you don't get anywhere by being so awkward.
CHESNEAU: Awkward?
JUDD: Lately you've become very loud. Whether you're right or wrong, it's not very effective. You're not going to make anyone want to change their mind. Jack Ockham, for God's sake, he's as eager to start the evacuation as you are. More eager. But he also knows the way to persuade the

Ambassador is never going to be by raising his voice. I'm
not quite sure why you do it. What your motives are for
this bitterness, Bob. It's self-indulgent. And it doesn't
have the effect you require.
(*There is a pause.*)
I say this from personal friendship.
CHESNEAU: (*Quietly*) Is this what everyone feels?

55. INT. BANK. DAY
The bank besieged with people desperate to trade their piastres.
Much argument with tellers. People behind the counters working
flat out. A TELLER *brings a packet to* BARBARA's *desk where she is*
working.
TELLER: This has been delivered by hand.
BARBARA: Thank you.
(*The* TELLER *goes.* BARBARA *looks at the packet, opens its top,*
takes the merest second's glance, then gets up and goes over to
another of the tellers, a girl of 17 on a high stool. At once
LHAN *gets up and follows* BARBARA *to a small filing office at*
the side of the main hall.)
Lhan, come in here. . . .

56. INT. FILING OFFICE. DAY
Continuous. They go in, BARBARA *closing the door, then she takes*
the packet and empties it out on a small table.
LHAN: Thank you.
(*Inside the packet are an air ticket and a passport which*
BARBARA *hands across, as she looks in the ticket.*)
BARBARA: Here's your passport as well.
LHAN: Thank you, Miss Dean.
(LHAN *is delighted. She gestures outside.*)
I have the dollars.
BARBARA: That's all right. You'll need them where you're
going. The flight is today. You must leave the bank early.
LHAN: All right.
(*She takes the ticket from* BARBARA. *Then pauses.*)
Miss Dean, I have an aunt. Also . . . she has two brothers.

51

(BARBARA *looks at her a moment, then leans across and kisses her with great affection. Then she leaves the room, but not encouragingly.*)

BARBARA: Leave their names. I'll see what I can do.

57. INT. SHREDDING ROOM. DAY

At once a great noise as OCKHAM *moves down a line of eight paper-shredders which are being fed continuously with thousands of documents, which are being unloaded by teams of assistants. We are in a large filing room, almost like a steel vault, whose contents have been ransacked and poured out on to the floor. As* OCKHAM *moves down the line, assistants come up to him with individual bundles for his personal approval.*

OCKHAM: Yeah, all that. (*He looks briefly at the next bundle.*) Get rid of it. (*The next.*) Yeah. Yeah. Sure, that as well. Anything with names we got to get rid of it. (*He speaks even before the next assistant has reached him.*) If it's got names, then it must go.

58. INT. INCINERATOR ROOM. DAY

An inferno of heat and noise. A terrible whine from the machines. Three men dressed only in trousers are shovelling piles of shredded paper into the incinerators. There are carts of shredded paper waiting to go. The fire inside is fierce. OCKHAM *stands near the men, shouting at the top of his voice to be heard.*

OCKHAM: It's hot.

MAN: Yeah. Ventilation. (*He points up to the ceiling.*) I don't think it's working.

(OCKHAM *nods. Then gestures at the great piles of paper.*)

OCKHAM: I'm afraid this is only the beginning. Just keep going as long as you can.

59. INT. OCKHAM'S OFFICE. DAY

OCKHAM *is now sitting at his desk downstairs. Round the door appears a very Ivy League State Department* YOUNG MAN, *nervous, in a suit.* OCKHAM *looks up.*

YOUNG MAN: I'm sorry, sir. It's the Ambassador. He says can you turn the incinerators off?

(OCKHAM *frowns*.)

He says he's sorry, but please can you do it?

(*The* YOUNG MAN *looks nervously at* OCKHAM.)

He says the ash is falling on the pool.

60. INT. BANK. NIGHT

QUOC *is sitting alone with the ledgers in the deserted bank. He is at his desk, in the back area.* BARBARA *appears in front of him, very still.*

BARBARA: Quoc. I'm afraid I sent Lhan off today.

QUOC: Yes, that's all right. She told me she would go.

(BARBARA *nods slightly*.)

BARBARA: I wanted to ask . . . if you would like me to help you.

QUOC: No.

(*There is a pause.* QUOC *stares at her impassively.*)

BARBARA: I felt I must ask.

QUOC: Whatever happens, I am staying in my country. My
family, my life is here.

BARBARA: But you hate the Communists.

QUOC: No, I don't hate them, I fear them, that's all.

(*She looks at him as if about to say something important.*)

BARBARA: The bank will trade until the last moment.

QUOC: Yes of course.

BARBARA: I needed to say. . . .

(*She stops, unable to express herself. She puts her hand suddenly over her mouth.* QUOC *seems simply to wait. She sees this and turns away.*)

Well, I'm sorry, I shouldn't have disturbed you. (*She turns to go.*) Goodnight, Quoc.

QUOC: Goodnight, Miss Dean.

61. INT. SITUATION ROOM. NIGHT

A group of senior Embassy men in the situation room. In the DAO's office inside the Embassy. It is late at night. The maps on the walls are dramatically lit by neon. At the centre of the room, surrounded by senior military, the AMBASSADOR *sits in deep gloom.* CHESNEAU *sits near* OCKHAM. *The* OFFICER *at the wall has just finished reporting from a large map of Military Region Three.*

OFFICER: I'm sorry, sir. There is nothing in the military situation which gives any grounds for hope. I would say . . . Saigon is encircled. At any moment the attack can be pressed home. (*He waits a moment, then tries to go on.*) In a way, I don't quite know why they're waiting . . .

AMBASSADOR: They're waiting because they still want to talk. (*His voice is barely raised.*) Why fight your way in when you can negotiate? They don't want to see this city destroyed. (*There is a silence. He is plainly on his own, yet no one wants to speak.* OCKHAM *leads quietly.*)

OCKHAM: Well, in that case, there's a precondition. Something we've discussed here before. For many years. It is a condition that the North will not negotiate unless President Thieu is removed.

AMBASSADOR: And it is of course I who must do it. (*There is a pause.*) Oh yes, Jack. *I* must hold the knife. (*Everyone looks at him in concealed astonishment. The military stare as he goes on.*) This man who's been loyal to us. A cup of bitterness. And you are all so keen I should drink. (OCKHAM *looks down, embarrassed.*)

OCKHAM: Well, it does seem . . . if we want to negotiate . . .

AMBASSADOR: Oh yes, of course, sound reasons I'm sure. (*He gets up from the chair and moves across the room, muttering. Then he turns and faces them.*) Well, so be it. It's what you've always wanted. All of you. Well . . . you have your way. (*He looks down to the floor. There is a silence.*)

CHESNEAU: (*Neutrally, not intimidated*) Does that mean, sir, we can start to evacuate? (*The* AMBASSADOR *turns and looks at him.*)

AMBASSADOR: Oh yes, Chesneau. Let hell come down.

62. INT. BAR. NIGHT

A rundown bar in the centre of town. Behind the bar the TV is on and Thieu is addressing the nation in obviously historic terms. At the bar

in a line sit CHESNEAU, JOAN MACKINTOSH, FRANK JUDD *and* BRAD,
a middle-aged American industrialist. CHESNEAU *gets down from his
stool and passes the television as he goes to the phone. He dials.*
CHESNEAU: Barbara. It's Bob.
BARBARA: (VO) Hello.
CHESNEAU: Are you watching?

63. INT. APARTMENT. NIGHT
In BARBARA's *darkened apartment the trunks have been pulled to the
centre of the room, and her belongings are half packed into them. She
is sitting on the edge of the bed and in the room distantly you can see
the same flickering image on the TV behind her—Thieu in black and
white.*
BARBARA: Yes. The television's on.
CHESNEAU: (VO) The Ambassador went to get rid of him this
    morning. He still seems to think it's going to help him get
    talks.
    (BARBARA *is staring ahead, detached.*)
BARBARA: Does that mean . . .?
CHESNEAU: (VO) Yeah. We start the big evacuation. All our
    effort's now to get people out.
    (BARBARA *does not react. He goes on with false enthusiasm.*)
    (VO) The wraps are really off. It's really beginning.
BARBARA: Ah well, good.
CHESNEAU: (VO) Yes. Well, we're pleased.
    (*Pause.* BARBARA *waiting.* CHESNEAU's *voice changes tone.*)
    (VO) Barbara, are you planning . . . are you going to leave
    yet?
BARBARA: No. (*She looks down.*) I've nothing. I've no life out
    there. Also . . . Bob. . . . (*Her need is suddenly naked.*) I
    miss you . . . can we meet?

64. INT. BAR. NIGHT
Continuous. CHESNEAU *stands by the bar, turned away from the
others, phone in hand, listening. He pauses a moment.*
CHESNEAU: I'd like to see you. But I have to go to the airport
    tonight.

65. EXT. OCKHAM'S HOUSE. NIGHT

OCKHAM's *house seen from the front in the near darkness, late at night. Just a glint of light on the front steps and into it at once steps a short, beautifully dressed dandy. He stops a moment. It is* THIEU. *Then* CHESNEAU's *voice from the dark, tactful.*

CHESNEAU: Sir.

> (*Behind* THIEU, *unseen in the dark, a couple of bodyguards whisper quietly but urgently.* THIEU *nods and moves down the steps, out of the light. At once we see a black car drawn up in the driveway.* JUDD *holding the back door open. The small figure gets silently into the car.* JUDD *goes round the back and closes the trunk, which is crammed with many fine leather suitcases.* CHESNEAU *is waiting at the passenger door and the two of them get into the seats, slipping in like French gangsters.* CHESNEAU *starts the engine. Then looks in his rear mirror where he can see* THIEU's *face staring straight ahead.*)

CHESNEAU: Sir, if you could . . . if you could just keep down. . . .

66. EXT. STREET. NIGHT

The black car moving smoothly through the now silent curfewed streets. The only moving object on a still landscape. As it goes by we see JUDD *and* CHESNEAU, *but the back is apparently empty.*

67. INT. CAR. NIGHT

CHESNEAU *intent on driving, looking around.* JUDD *beside him looks in the mirror, shifts slightly.*

JUDD: (*Quietly*) Are you, em . . . are you going to join your family, sir?

> (THIEU's *voice from the floor of the back of the car.*)

THIEU: No. They are buying antiques. (*He nods judiciously, then looks quickly at* CHESNEAU, *alert for trouble from outside.*) They have already gone to London.

> (*We see* THIEU *for the first time. He is sitting on the floor of the car, right down at the back. His two bodyguards are squeezed beside him.* JUDD's *voice.*)

JUDD: (VO) London's nice at this time of year.

56

68. INT. GYMNASIUM. DAY

A wide shot of the huge empty gymnasium which the DOA will use as evacuation headquarters. It is almost empty but for some trestle tables which stand waiting, stacked at the side of the building. Old basketball nets hang from the ceiling.

BARBARA: (VO) So it began, the delayed evacuation. . . .

69. INT. GYMNASIUM. DAY

FIEDLER *at the centre of the gym. Now teams of marines all around as he describes how he wants everything laid out.*

FIEDLER: Tables. . . . Lines of applications. . . . Vietnamese
    exit papers over there. . . .
    (*With each instruction he gestures hugely.*)

70. INT. GYMNASIUM. DAY

The scene being transformed. Tables being set up. Men arriving with temporary office equipment. Catering equipment passed hand to hand along a human chain. FIEDLER *on the move, pointing to where everything is to go, receiving attendant soldiers as they come to him for instruction.*

BARBARA: (VO) Out at the airport they transformed the gym . . .
    (FIEDLER *points to one corner.*)

FIEDLER: Kitchens. (*Then to a pile of equipment.*) Gas burners. (*He
    points again.*) Toilet facilities. . . .
    (*A* SOLDIER *has come up to him, pointing to a fresh mound of PX goods.*)

SOLDIER: Sir, this is three hundredweight of franks and beans.
    (*They stand, laughing easily.*)

71. INT. GYMNASIUM. DAY

The scene transformed completely. Tables set out in immaculate rows. Men waiting behind them to receive the lines. Ropes set out to define the lines. Kitchen staff waiting with gleaming equipment. In the space of a few hours, a perfect logistical operation has been finished, and the team for the job now stands waiting.

BARBARA: (VO) They built a facility they called Dodge City.
    (FIEDLER *at the centre of the room turns to an attendant officer.*)

FIEDLER: OK, everyone. Open the doors.

PART THREE

72. INT. TAXI. DAY

Fade-up. BARBARA *in the back of a taxi going through the streets of Saigon. They are very crowded. On the sidewalks people are gathering round the street traders, who have huge piles of goods stacked around them.*

BARBARA: (VO) The last few days the streets were always busy . . . all the objects people needed to unload. . . .
(*We watch the sidewalks going by from behind the glass.*)
Wherever you went, air-conditioning units . . . fridges . . . televisions . . . stoves. . . .

73. INT. APARTMENT. DAY

BARBARA's *apartment now cleared out. The luggage neatly stacked at the centre of the room. Around the walls and shelves have been cleared. On a rail in the corner of the room there are still a few dresses and* BARBARA *is now handing one to her* MAID.

BARBARA: Have this, OK?

MAID: Yes, thank you.
(*She holds it up delightedly against her body.*)
Hey, it's good, it really looks good . . .
(BARBARA *looks at her a moment.*)

BARBARA: You know it means that soon I'll be leaving?

MAID: Oh yes.
(*The* MAID *turns with unconcern, and stands delightedly with a mirror.*)
Hey, I'm going to look good.

74. INT. CERCLE SPORTIF. DAY

BARBARA *in the women's locker room at the Cercle Sportif. It is deserted. Grey ranks of closets. She has opened her locker and is pouring old tennis gear on to the floor.*

BARBARA: (VO) Suddenly at last the Cercle Sportif was
    deserted. . . .

75. EXT. CERCLE SPORTIF. DAY

A few solitary Frenchmen in chic costumes sit by the large, slightly green pool with doric pillars behind. The odd servant brings them iced drinks. They read Le Monde.

BARBARA: (VO) Only the French still sit by the pool. . . . As if
    the Americans had only come briefly and the French had
    never expected they would stay.

76. INT. CERCLE SPORTIF. DAY

BARBARA *sitting alone with a drink, staring out, in the part where we earlier saw them playing cards. A waiter comes across with a bunch of roses. She is suddenly beginning to look old.*

BARBARA: (VO) The Foreign Minister I'd played bridge with
    sent me roses. Later I found out he'd already gone. . . .
    (*She smiles up at the waiter, puts the flowers carelessly aside.*)
    (VO) Like so many . . . without any warning. The
    Americans got him away in the night.

77. INT. GYMNASIUM. DAY

The gym, transformed again. Now crammed with evacuees in long lines, some of whom have been sleeping on the spot, waiting for their turn for their applications to be processed. The place is patrolled at the side by GIs in olive drab. JUDD *is pushing his way through the crowd with a short* VIETNAMESE *of about 45, who has an overstuffed suitcase. He is trying to reach* COLONEL FIEDLER *who is still at the centre of things, but by now worn down, frazzled.* JUDD *has to shout to make himself heard.*

JUDD: Colonel, I'm wondering. . . . This is a friend of mine.

FIEDLER: Everyone seems to have so many friends.

JUDD: He's a tailor. He made shirts for the Embassy.

(FIEDLER *looks at him a moment, then turns to* JUDD.)

FIEDLER: Any idea why he's decided to go?

(JUDD *turns to the* TAILOR *and speaks to him in Vietnamese. As he answers,* JUDD *translates*.)

JUDD: Everyone else is going . . . all his friends have already left.

FIEDLER: Yeah, OK. . . .

(*He looks at the* VIETNAMESE *hopelessly*.)

Well, why not then?

(*He reaches across for a couple of exit papers from an officer's pile on a nearby table*.)

Tell him he may have to wait for a while.

78. INT. BANK. DAY

The bank as normal, peaceful now, in contrast to the airport. Everything in its familiar place. BARBARA *working at her desk.* QUOC *appears beside her*.

QUOC: Miss Dean, I'm afraid we have lost Mr Haliwell.

BARBARA: What?

(*He reaches out with an envelope*.)

QUOC: He asked to pass you on this.

(*She looks up, then goes and opens the door of Haliwell's office*.)

79. INT. OFFICE. DAY

The office is empty. The desk cleared. The ledgers in a tidy pile at the side of the desk. The Times *still in its place. A coat hangs on the coat rack.* BARBARA *moves into the office, reading the letter.* QUOC *follows her in*.

QUOC: He went for lunch and he left you this message.

BARBARA: Yes.

(*She has opened it. Inside there is a note and an airline ticket. She looks at the ticket, then turns as if to resume normality*.)

Well, thank you, Quoc.

(QUOC *lingers, surprised he is being dismissed*.)

QUOC: Are you leaving?

BARBARA: What?

QUOC: Will you follow him?

(*She looks at him a moment*.)

BARBARA: What do you think I should do?

(QUOC *raises his eyebrows slightly*.)

QUOC: I would say yes. It will come anyway. Better you do it as soon as you can.

80. INT. BANK. DAY

The back area. Everyone diligently at work, as QUOC *and* BARBARA *come out of Haliwell's office. She makes for the desk, pauses a moment, reaches for the cardigan which is draped round the back of the chair.*

QUOC: No, leave that. It is less suspicious.

(*She nods and begins to move away*.)

BARBARA: Yes.

QUOC: But your handbag . . . if you want cigarettes . . .

(*He is pointing to the bag which is left on the chair.* BARBARA *realizes and dips down to pick it up*.)

BARBARA: Yes. Thank you.

QUOC: No. You are welcome.

(*They stand looking at each other*.)

BARBARA: Goodbye, Quoc.

QUOC: Goodbye, Miss Dean.

81. INT. BANK. DAY

At once a high shot of the bank at work. BARBARA *walking quickly down the stairs and out the main door.*

82. INT. CORRIDOR. DAY

The busy corridor at the CIA Headquarters, fifth floor. CHESNEAU *is coming down the corridor. He is wearing a helmet, and his hand is stuffed with papers.* JUDD *is coming from the other direction, also in a helmet.*

CHESNEAU: What's the news?

JUDD: There's been a second ultimatum. It says all US personnel must withdraw. . . .

(*They keep on moving together towards the offices*.)

If we don't get out there's going to be bloodshed. . . . (*He turns back ironically*.) The Ambassador says they still want to talk.

83. INT. OFFICE. DAY

The office is as busy as ever, but all the secretaries who are otherwise dressed normally are wearing helmets. The effect is very odd. As soon as she sees him coming through, LINDA *gets up to talk to* CHESNEAU, *who is coming in talking to* JUDD.

CHESNEAU: *And* we're expecting an attack on the airport . . .

LINDA: Bob . . .

> (CHESNEAU *nods to* JUDD *that he'll join him in a minute, recognizing the seriousness of* LINDA's *tone. She silently nods him over to the quiet corner of the office. They go to a filing cabinet which has a Thomson sub-machine-gun lying incongruously on top of it.*)

There's a woman downstairs.

> (CHESNEAU *frowns.*)

The woman who came with you . . .

CHESNEAU: Ah yes.

> (*He stands a moment, not knowing what to do.*)

LINDA: . . . last Christmas . . .

> (*He nods.*)

CHESNEAU: Put her in a room. I'll be down when I can.

84. INT. EMBASSY. DAY

BARBARA *is walked down the ground-floor passage of the Embassy by two Marines. They open a door, and inside is a deserted office, which has been cleared. It is empty.* BARBARA *goes in. The walls are decorated by pictures of America, posters of the Rockies, Manhattan, etc.*

BARBARA: Thank you.

> (*The two men go, closing the door. She sits down, alone.*)

85. INT. BANK. DAY

QUOC *sitting at his desk, as usual. The work of the bank going on. A couple of tellers laughing, during the slack period. Then a third teller signals to* QUOC *to come over. A young* AMERICAN WOMAN *is at the other side of the counter.*

WOMAN: I'm so sorry. I need my credit cleared. Is the manager here?

QUOC: Yes of course. I'll just speak to him. (*He reaches through the guichet and takes her cheque book.*) Will you hold on a moment, please?
(*We see him walk into the manager's office, having tapped three times on the door. He goes in. A pause. The tellers chatter, oblivious. Then after a few moments he comes out again, closing the door behind him. He rejoins the tellers and customer.*)
The manager says, yes, we can pay on this. (*He pushes the book back.*) Would you like to make out your cheque?

86. EXT. EMBASSY. NIGHT
The American Embassy seen from outside. The huge white building. The night is silent around it, but high in the building lights burn.

87. INT. OCKHAM'S OFFICE. NIGHT
A very low-key briefing, dead of night. OCKHAM *at his desk, the few trusted analysts around the room.* OCKHAM *tired. There are cans of Heineken on his desk.*
OCKHAM: The North is going to give us twenty-four hours. It's been negotiated. That's how long they're willing to hold off. Washington is insisting no phoney heroics. We are only to take essential locals with us at the end.
CHESNEAU: What does that mean?
OCKHAM: It means what we want it to, Bob. (*He smiles, bitterly.*) They've never known anything of what it's like here. (*He looks down, uncharacteristically emotional.*) Meanwhile please . . . your work is nearly over. I'd advise you all to try and get some sleep.

88. INT. EMBASSY. NIGHT
BARBARA *asleep in a chair in the Embassy office.* CHESNEAU *standing over her in the near dark. She looks abandoned.* CHESNEAU *speaks to her asleep.*
CHESNEAU: I'm sorry, I was working.
(*She wakes. Looks at him. Smiles.*)
BARBARA: What?
CHESNEAU: I didn't forget you.

BARBARA: I couldn't face leaving.

CHESNEAU: No, it's all right.

BARBARA: Haliwell went . . .

CHESNEAU: In that case he must have caught the last plane.
    (CHESNEAU *moves away.*)
    The airport's gone.
    (BARBARA *in real panic looks across at him.*)

BARBARA: Oh Bob, have I been very stupid?

CHESNEAU: No. You can helicopter out. The Jolly Green Giants.
    We're bringing them into downtown Saigon.
    (BARBARA *looks at him, puzzled.*)

BARBARA: But how do you know . . .?

CHESNEAU: There's an agreement. They're giving us exactly
    twenty-four hours. And everyone's ready. All American
    citizens have been issued with assembly points. (*He smiles.*)
    They're waiting for a signal.
    (BARBARA *smiles also, in anticipation.*)

BARBARA: You play 'White Christmas'?

CHESNEAU: Yes. They're serious.

BARBARA: I thought it was a joke.

CHESNEAU: It's a joke. It's serious as well.
    (*They smile at each other, the old humour between them, the old
    tone of voice.*)
    The radio station plays Bing Crosby, and all Americans
    know it's the end.

89. EXT. EMBASSY COMPOUND. NIGHT

*The empty compound outside the Embassy streaked with searchlights
which are now on for the night. The noise of gunfire has now died.
From the dark, running very lightly, come two GIs and an OFFICER,
making for a huge tree which dominates the compound. One GI
stumbles slightly as he reaches it.*

FIRST GI: Shit.

OFFICER: Keep it quiet.

SECOND GI: How the hell. . . ? (*He gestures despairingly at the huge
    chainsaw he is carrying.*) There's no way he ain't going to
    hear it.

OFFICER: It's the Ambassador's favourite tree.
(*The* FIRST GI *makes a signal of despair and looks up at the great branches of the tamarind. The* OFFICER *shrugs.*)
We've gotta do it. We need the landing space. (*He nods at the* SECOND GI.) Nothing for it. Let's go.
(*The two men start the chainsaw. The petrol motor is deafening.*)
Jesus.
(*It bites into the trunk. At once, at a high window, way up on the top floor of the Embassy, the stricken figure of the* AMBASSADOR *appears, like a prisoner shouting from behind his bullet-proof glass.*)
AMBASSADOR: What the hell is going on here?

90. INT. APARTMENT. DAY
There are some bags, packed, in the centre of the room. CHESNEAU *stand alone in the living room. He is looking at his watch. It says 7:45.* BARBARA *is out of sight, gathering stuff from the bedroom. She calls to him from there.*
BARBARA: Nearly ready.
CHESNEAU: It's OK.
BARBARA: I'm sorry, I'm taking your time up.
CHESNEAU: No. (*He stands, patient. Then almost to himself*) Go your own speed.
(*For the first time* BARBARA *appears, by the door jamb. She holds a few random objects she is planning to pack.*)
BARBARA: Do you want to go?
CHESNEAU: Yeah, there'll be choppers at the Embassy.
BARBARA: And what . . . you think I should get on?
CHESNEAU: Well sure, I mean . . .
BARBARA: No I meant . . . you mean *now*? Or can't I hang on for you?
(*A pause, he does not reply.*)
I've never even asked where the helicopter takes me.
CHESNEAU: To the Philippines.
(*He smiles slightly, but already she is going on with a new urgency.*)
BARBARA: Listen, I have a friend. A terrific girl. She used to

65

bring me laundry. Put her on. She's a wonderful girl.
Let her go in my place.
(*He is still looking at her.*)
Why not? Just the chance to be with you.
(*She turns away.*)
It's the waste. All the time we've wasted.

CHESNEAU: Yes, I know. That was my fault.
(*He moves across the room. She is in his arms.*)
When I first came here, Barbara, I thought I could do this job decently. I thought it was honourable work. And even now I'm not ashamed, all the work we've done, this week, all the people I've managed to get out. But also it's the nature of the thing. It's been left to us. 'Hey, you guys, go and make us look good.' Well, we didn't. We weren't any better at losing the war than we were at winning it. And Barbara . . . you made it worse for me. Every time I saw you, you made me feel guilty. I couldn't take that after a while. That's why I stopped coming to see you. (*Tenderly*) Now it seems stupid. Now that we're here.
(*They embrace. There is a pause.*)

BARBARA: It's so strange. Everywhere you go you hear people saying 'Oh I loved this country.' That's what they say. They usually say it just as they're leaving. 'Oh I loved this country so much . . .' I realized when I was in the bank one evening. This was . . . oh some time ago. I tried to say something affectionate to Quoc. Well, that's what you're left with. Gestures of affection. Which you then find mean nothing at all.

CHESNEAU: (*Moved*) Barbara, please . . .
(*But she at once moves past him, leaving the room.*)

BARBARA: Put me on a helicopter!

CHESNEAU: Barbara . . .

BARBARA: Shut up! Put me on!
(*She leaves the room. A silence.* CHESNEAU, *left alone, stunned by this sudden change.*
We cut to BARBARA *in the bathroom. She is putting her toilet things into a sponge bag.* CHESNEAU *appears behind her at the door.*)

CHESNEAU: What will you do? Will you go back to England?

BARBARA: My mother.

CHESNEAU: May I come and see you there?

(*She turns and looks at him as if the idea were self-evidently absurd. Then she quietly tips the cosmetics into the sink and leaves them behind.*)

BARBARA: I think let's leave the place to be looted. Don't you think so?

(*She goes from the bathroom. She goes from the main room, leaving her bag behind on the floor.*)

CHESNEAU: Sure, if you want.

91. EXT. STREET. DAY

CHESNEAU *comes quickly down the stairs carrying* BARBARA's *luggage urgently now to the car. As he puts it down he looks up into the sky, and we cut to the helicopters arriving overhead. Marine helicopters are now flying overhead into the city.*

CHESNEAU *and* BARBARA *drive together through the streets. As they pass along a shopping street, they see the old South Vietnamese flags being pulled down, and the flags of the new regime being put up.*

As their car draws closer to the Embassy, they overtake straggling lines of Americans who are walking with their suitcases down the road towards the compound.

92. INT. CAR. DAY

Inside the car the radio is playing 'White Christmas' as BARBARA *watches the stragglers in the street.*

BARBARA: Look! Coming in on signal . . .

(CHESNEAU *smiles. The crowd begins to thicken as they approach the Embassy. They pass burning and wrecked-out cars. As they get near the gate they see a huge crowd.* BARBARA *points to the thickest part.*)

Look! Over there!

93. EXT. EMBASSY GATE. DAY

Outside the Embassy in the huge crowd, HALIWELL *is desperately*

67

*trying to push his way through. He is carrying a suitcase, lost in a
hostile crowd.*

HALIWELL: English! English! Please I'm English! English! Please
let me through!

94. INT. CAR. DAY

BARBARA *desperately trying to catch sight of him through the crowd.*
CHESNEAU *trying to edge the car towards him through the crowd, who
are now beginning to turn ugly. They bang on the roof. They hit the
side of the car with their fists.*

BARBARA: He must have got caught at the airport.

CHESNEAU: Hold on. Let me try. . . .

95. EXT. STREET. DAY

*The first great helicopter hovers over the Embassy to make its way
down into the compound. At once the crowd begins to push even
harder, packing in a press towards the gate.*

HALIWELL: English! English!

  (*In the excitement he is pushed to the ground. Some random rifle
  shots are fired in the air. People scream.* CHESNEAU *draws
  alongside* HALIWELL.)

CHESNEAU: Quick. Get him in.

  (BARBARA *reaches for the door and opens it, as* CHESNEAU
  stretches right across the seats and pulls HALIWELL *like a
  beached whale into the car. He turns back to the wheel, while*
  BARBARA *closes the door.*)

HALIWELL: My God!

CHESNEAU: Close the door!

  (BARBARA *slams it as the car is inched towards the gates.*)

HALIWELL: Oh God, for a moment out there . . .

  (*He stops, checking himself,* BARBARA *looks at him. He tries to
  smile and shake his head. The gate is opened fractionally to
  allow* CHESNEAU'*s car into the compound.*)

CHESNEAU: Right, OK. We're getting there.

  (*We watch the crowd surging against the gate, the GIs holding
  them back with rifles.*)

BARBARA: For a moment you felt what it's like to be them.

96. EXT. COMPOUND. DAY

The tremendous circular cloud of dust going up as the first helicopter comes down with a great roar by the tree stump. Marines jump from the helicopter with guns as it lands. The crowd inside the compound, half white, half Asian, gathers round to get on. The GI is shouting above the noise.

FIRST GI: It's all right. Everyone's going. Please. Everyone. Just hold on.

> *(By the gate the far greater crowd is pressing much more urgently to get in. A man now flings himself at the gate in an attempt to climb over. At once a GI brings his rifle butt crashing down on his head.*
>
> *We cut back to the GI inside the compound.)*

Everyone OK. There will be a place for you. Everyone inside is going to get on.

97. INT. CORRIDOR. DAY

COLONEL FIEDLER *walking along the main corridor in fatigues and helmet. It is absolute chaos. The place has been ransacked as fast as possible to destroy as much equipment and papers as possible. People are running back and forth with stuff for the incinerators. The* COLONEL *is simply opening the door of each room and shouting inside.*

COLONEL: All right, please, let's get on with it. Everyone out. We're all going home.

> *(He comes into the communal office, now ravaged by the speed of the exit.* LINDA *and the others are still working in helmets, piling stuff out of cabinets on to the floor.)*

All women first. Hey—

> *(He smiles at* LINDA. *The mood is good-hearted.)*

Out please. *(Then a military joke.)* Everyone, please, in orderly lines.

98. INT. PASSAGEWAY. DAY

At the end of a concrete passageway you can see teams of people, about forty in all, feeding papers into the burners in the distance. They are scorched with effort. At the front there is a SOLDIER *hauling a big bag along, single-handed. He is stopped by an* OFFICER.

OFFICER: Soldier, what's that?

SOLDIER: It's two million dollars, sir.

(*The* OFFICER *looks at him.*)

It's the Ambassador's emergency fund.

OFFICER: Where's it going?

SOLDIER: I've orders to burn it.

(*The* OFFICER *nods, and casually reaches into the bag, takes out a handful of dollars and stuffs them into the* MAN's *hand.*)

OFFICER: All right, soldier. I'll see to that.

99. EXT. COMPOUND. DAY

The crowd gathered at the helicopter. We watch the COMMANDING OFFICER *at work, striding round the area.*

COMMANDING OFFICER: OK here, please. Yeah. You here. OK, yeah.

(*The* MARINE *inside the helicopter yells across.*)

MARINE: That's all we can take.

(CHESNEAU *appears at the* OFFICER's *side.*)

CHESNEAU: Bill, I've two friends.

OFFICER: Sure, put 'em on then.

(CHESNEAU *turns back. At the front of the crowd,* BARBARA *and* HALIWELL *are standing together.*)

CHESNEAU: Barbara!

(*They make their way past the crowd to the helicopter.*

HALIWELL *gets on.* CHESNEAU *holds a moment with* BARBARA.)

Good luck, OK?

(*As they stand looking, the* OFFICER *passes them impatiently.*)

OFFICER: Come on, please.

(*And* CHESNEAU *steps back, yells to the helicopter.*)

CHESNEAU: Goodbye, Mr Haliwell.

BARBARA: God, have I really got to get on to this thing?

(*She is muttering to herself as she makes her way.* CHESNEAU *waves to* HALIWELL *inside.*)

OFFICER: OK, everyone, please—let's lift it.

(*The crowd falls back.*)

Stand by. Everyone clear.

(*She is sitting opposite the open main door of the helicopter, next to* HALIWELL, *as it begins to go up. She is wearing a panama hat. She is an old English spinster. The image rises into the air and out of the frame as we hear the voice of the* OFFICER.)

Next lot, OK? Right. Get ready. You. You and you, right? Right. Over there.

100. INT. OFFICE. DAY

CHESNEAU *with an axe is now attacking the laminated maps on the walls of his office. They are absolutely covered with the red scrawls of the advancing army. He is making wild swings to cut the wood they are mounted on. Systematically taking his own anger out.* JUDD *arrives, alarmed by the noise.*

JUDD: God almighty, what the hell are you doing?

(CHESNEAU *turns smiling.*)

CHESNEAU: How do you suggest I get rid of these things?

JUDD: If we had any sense, we'd just set fire to it, we'd burn the whole place down.

(*He turns hopelessly to survey the amount of paper still left in the office.* CHESNEAU *has pulled the drawer out of a filing cabinet. It is full of plastic individual name cards, several thousand. Each with a person's name on it.*)

CHESNEAU: What about these? People's name plates . . . agents who worked for us. . . .

(*From the drawer he also takes duplicated foolscap sheets, all with lists of names.*)

Lists. All the people we promised to get out . . .

(OCKHAM *appears at the door.*)

OCKHAM: Oh Bob, could you come . . .?

CHESNEAU: Yeah . . .

(OCKHAM *waves airily as he goes.*)

OCKHAM: Just leave that. . . .

(*As he goes out the main office,* CHESNEAU *sets the drawer full of names and lists down on a desk.*)

We've got problems with helicopter sites.

(*They go out. We pause a moment on the drawer* CHESNEAU *has abandoned on the desktop.*)

A line of people being passed hand to hand up a dangerous chain that leads to the very top of the Embassy where a COMPOUND OFFICER *then handles them into the helicopter on top. Next to him is the* OFFICER *with two million dollars.*

They shout.

BAG OFFICER: This doesn't look good.

COMPOUND OFFICER: The ground's too dangerous.

> (*He points down to the compound where the crowd are now looking up towards the roof. Around them the gates are still besieged.*)

We got frightened of killing the gooks.

> (BAG OFFICER *nods. And then he puts his hand on the* COMPOUND OFFICER's *shoulder, as he steps into the line to leave. The* COMPOUND OFFICER *frowns slightly at the size of his bag.*)

You taking that?

BAG OFFICER: Yeah, I have to.

> (*The* COMPOUND OFFICER *moves round to signal to the pilot.*)

COMPOUND OFFICER: OK. Right. Lift away.

> (*He holds both thumbs up. In an immensely precarious movement, the Green Giant lifts off. As it does, it tilts to one side. We just catch sight of the* BAG OFFICER, *desperately grabbing at the bag as it slides across the floor. As the helicopter gains height, the bag falls. Thousands and thousands of dollars flutter out of the air.*
>
> *The crowd in the compound looks up as the money flutters down on them and into the pool.*)

102. INT. SCHOOL. EVENING

A Vietnamese schoolroom. Two hundred people sitting patiently on the classroom floor with their baggage, while in the headmaster's small office off the main room, an American in late middle age is sitting on the table with a telephone. We recognize him from the Tu Do bar earlier. He has a saddlebag. As he speaks he looks to the crowds, cramped and patient on the floor.

BRAD: Jack, it's Brad.

OCKHAM: (VO) Yeah.

BRAD: Brad at Forbes Chemicals.

OCKHAM: (VO) Yeah, I know who you are.

BRAD: I'm with my designated employees. Jack, we've been
waiting six hours.
(*He looks out to the playground which is cleared and empty, as
if waiting for a landing.*)
We're at our assembly point, but nobody's come for us. All
the choppers are flying right by.
(*There's a slight pause at the other end.*)

OCKHAM: Yeah, that's right. They're on their way to you.

BRAD: We've decided to make it through town. I'm going to lead
them across to the Embassy . . .

OCKHAM: (VO) No, please, Brad. . . .

103. INT. OCKHAM'S OFFICE. EVENING

Continuous. OCKHAM *exhausted at his desk. His office is ravaged.
The contents have been cleared by Marines who are still working to
take things out. The remains of the CIA corps, who number about
eight, are working around him on the phones ringing in the offices.
There is a great deal of drink—a crate of Heineken at the centre of
the room.*

OCKHAM: It's not a good idea.

BRAD: (VO) But, Jack . . .

OCKHAM: If you just hold on, we will come and get you. . . .
(*He turns and looks at* JUDD *who is talking on another phone.*)
The crowd's getting ugly, you must stay where you are.

JUDD: (*Simultaneously*) No, they're coming, I promise you . . .
(CHESNEAU *drops a scrawled note across the desk to* JUDD.)

CHESNEAU: Another two hundred waiting in Cholon.
(JUDD *sees it but does not acknowledge it. Instead he picks up in
his other hand a phone which is ringing and, while he talks to
the first source, cuts the second phone off by pressing down on
the cradle.*)

JUDD: It's OK. You will be collected.
(*Then he drops the newly dead line into the waste-paper basket*)
Nobody is going to get left behind.

104. INT. BANK. NIGHT

QUOC *alone in the bank, closing the shutters with the long pole. It is eerily dark and quiet. Then he walks back across the deserted bank and picks up his briefcase which he puts under his arm. Then he goes to the door and, without looking back, goes out.*

105. INT. WASHROOM. NIGHT

The AMBASSADOR *stands washing his hands, then dries them carefully and walks out of the washroom into the deserted corridor.*

106. INT. CORRIDOR. NIGHT

He walks along the corridor and goes into his office. The corridor is deserted.

107. INT. OFFICE. NIGHT

He walks through his outer office which is now unmanned and goes into his own inner office. It is similarly deserted. He goes to the American flag which is pinned on the wall and now unpins it. He takes it from the wall and folds it into the shape of a tea towel. Then he puts it in a plastic bag which he has left on his desk. He then picks up a cable from his desk and with the bag and the cable leaves the room.

108. INT. CORRIDOR. NIGHT

The corridor which only a moment ago was deserted is now full of the remaining staff who number about twelve in all. They have appeared while the AMBASSADOR *has been in his office and are now waiting for him in the corridor. He is haggard, he has flu, he looks terrible. He reads them the cable.*

AMBASSADOR: Gentlemen. This is from the President. The Ambassador is ordered to leave. (*He looks down.*) We are withdrawing the American presence under orders. (*He nods slightly and looks at them.*) Thanks very much.

109. INT. CORRIDOR. NIGHT

The whole group seemingly driven along the corridor by the stricken giant at their head. They keep close together as they walk through the

74

darkened building. OCKHAM *and* CHESNEAU *are at the back like straggling schoolboys who can't keep up on the walk. They whisper furiously to one another.*

CHESNEAU: What's going to happen to all those people?

OCKHAM: Bob, there's nothing . . .

CHESNEAU: There are thousands of them still at the assembly points. I tell you, they've been waiting all day.

OCKHAM: We can't, there's nothing. . . . (*There is a strange bump and clink in their progress.*)

Shit.

CHESNEAU: What's that?

OCKHAM: Whisky bottle.

(*A bottle has rolled out on to the floor from* OCKHAM'*s pocket, but they do not stop to pick it up. It is left there.*)

Face it, Bob. There's nothing we can do.

110. INT. CHESNEAU'S OFFICE. NIGHT

The group go past the open office door. We just catch their voices as they do.

CHESNEAU: But Jack . . . listen. . . .

(*A pause. The office ransacked, deserted. Then we adjust to settle in the foreground on the drawer full of agents' name plates, forgotten on the desk.*
We hold on that.)

111. INT. STAIRWELL. NIGHT

At the top landing as the group all reach it, the military are waiting already by the exit door at the top of the building to take the AMBASSADOR *out on the last flight.*

As the group reaches the small landing, the AMBASSADOR *turns to speak to the assembled company. He still holds his bag.*

AMBASSADOR: Gentlemen, before I leave I would like to . . .

(*A great cry from the bottom of the stairwell.*)

SOLDIER: Sir. Sir. Let's get the hell out.

(*The* AMBASSADOR *shocked by the voice of the panicking* SOLDIER.)

They're breaking into the Embassy.

AMBASSADOR: What?

SOLDIER: They've heard this is going to be the last flight.

    (*There is a second's indecision on the* AMBASSADOR's *face, then suddenly he gestures at the door.*)

AMBASSADOR: All right—out!

112. INT. EMBASSY. NIGHT.

At once the mad scramble is shown going on downstairs as the two GIs on guard desperately close the main doors to the Embassy against the crowd. Then they run across the lobby to where a third GI is waiting holding the door to the stairway open.

FIRST GI: OK, for fuck's sake lock it.

    (*The main doors being smashed open and the crowd pouring into the Embassy.*)

113. INT. STAIRWELL. NIGHT

At the top of the stairwell, the military and CIA scramble desperately out of the tiny exit door on the landing out to the waiting helicopter.

114. INT. STAIRWELL. NIGHT

One GI slamming the stairwell door and locking it while the other two run for the stairs.

115. EXT. ROOF. NIGHT

The waiting helicopters now loaded, waiting, blades turning. The door to the stairwell held open by the last OFFICER.

116. INT. STAIRWELL. NIGHT.

The last soldiers running up the stairs. Reaching the top. There are sounds of people coming up from below, but at once the GIs open gas canisters and throw them down the stairs at the approaching crowd. You catch a glimpse of them scampering through the door and it closing as the screen smokes out.

117. EXT. STREETS. NIGHT

The streets of Saigon. Night. Quiet. Nothing moves. Eerie. The sound of the helicopters has gone. The cathedral. The opera house. Tu Do deserted.

118. EXT. COMPOUND. NIGHT
The two hundred Vietnamese and BRAD *in the school compound,*
waiting, scanning the empty sky.

119. EXT. STREETS. NIGHT
A side street. Round the corner, jogging in a small group, come eight
soldiers in formation. They are in army uniform, with guns, in full
battledress. As they turn into the street, the group suddenly breaks up
and they stop. They put down their guns, and start to undress. They
put down their boots, guns, clothes, in small heaps on the pavement.
They stand a moment in their boxer shorts. Then turn, as casually as
they can, and disappear down the street.
The little puddles of clothes left behind them.

120. INT. HELICOPTER. NIGHT
Inside the helicopter the group has settled, cheerful. A false
exhilaration. CHESNEAU *is sitting next to* JUDD, *on one side.*
Suddenly he remembers.
CHESNEAU: Shit.
JUDD: What?
CHESNEAU: I've remembered . . .
    (JUDD *puzzled.*)
JUDD: What?
    (CHESNEAU *looks down, appalled, disturbed. Avoids the*
    question.)
CHESNEAU: Something.
JUDD: (*A joke*) Do you want to go back?
    (CHESNEAU *turns, looks back, the truth dawning on him of what*
    he has done.)
CHESNEAU: (*Under his breath*) God forgive us.
    (*Suddenly the* PILOT *turns and yells back from the controls, as a*
    can of Heineken is opened in front of him.)
PILOT: Hey, you guys. We're all going home!
    (*Fast fade.*)